# THE SMALL HOUSE BOOK

## JAY SHAFER

First published in the United States in 2009
by Tumbleweed Tiny House Company
Post Office Box 1907
Boyes Hot Springs, California 95416

www.tumbleweedhouses.com

Copyright 2009-2010 Tumbleweed Tiny House Company
ISBN 978-1-60743-564-8

Designed, photographed and written by Jay Shafer

Additonal photography by...
Povy Kendal Atchison, pages 14, 16 & 17
Janine Björnson, page 196
Mike Johns, pages 70-76
Greg Johnson, page 64
Jack Journey, pages 138-145, 148-155, 160-163, 188 & 189
Michael McGettigan, page 59
Marty Shafer, page 5
Mary Wolverton, pages 62 & 63

Cover image: The author's house superimposed onto the Russian River in Jenner, CA

# Contents

# Introduction

I live in a house smaller than some people's closets. My decision to inhabit just 90 square feet arose from some concerns I had about the impact a larger house would have on the environment and because I just do not want to maintain a lot of unused or unusable space. My house meets all of my domestic needs without demanding much in return. The simple, slower lifestyle it affords is a luxury for which I am continually grateful.

If smaller, well-designed houses aren't the wave of the future, they certainly are a significant ripple on that wave. On these pages, I explain why. I also share my personal experiences with living in diminutive homes, meeting codes, and designing small spaces that work.

This book is a revised edition of the one I published several years ago under the same title. To this edition, I've added a section on how to build your own tiny house and a portfolio of my own designs. I hope you enjoy it.

Sincerely,

Jay Shafer

Jay, at home.

5

*"There is only one success – to be able to spend your own life in your own way."*
-Christopher Morley

# PART ONE:
# CONFESSIONS OF A CLAUSTROPHILE

# Living Large in Small Spaces

## The Airstream

I have been living in houses of fewer than 100 square feet for nearly twelve years. The first of my little abodes was a fourteen-foot Airstream. I bought it in the summer of 1997 for three thousand dollars. It came as-is, with an aluminum shell as streamlined and polished as what lay inside was hideous. The 1964 orange shag, asbestos tiles, and green Formica would have to go.

I began gutting, then meticulously refurbishing the interior in August, and by October, I was sleeping with an aluminum roof over my head. The place looked like a barrel on the inside, with pine tongue-and-groove running from front-to-back and floor-to-vaulted ceiling.

I settled in on a tree-lined ridge at the edge of a friend's alfalfa field. It was a three-minute walk to Rapid Creek Road and a ten-minute drive from there to Iowa City. I carried water in from a well by the road and allowed it to drain from my sink and shower directly into the grass outside. I carried my sawdust toilet (i.e., bucket) out about once a month and took it to the sewage treatment facility in town. My electrical appliances consisted of a fan, six lights, a 9-inch TV/VCR and a small boom box. A single solar panel fed them all. It seemed that this simple existence would provide all I needed.

Then December came. I had reinforced most of the trailer's insulation, but some areas remained thin. I spent over a half-hour each morning, from Christmas until Valentine's Day, chipping ice and sponging up condensation from my walls, floors and desktop. This went on for a couple of winters before I began construction on the tiny house I have since come to call "Tumbleweed".

The Airstream's exterior...

... and interior.

# Tumbleweed

It was not until after I thought I had already finished designing my little dream home that I became familiar with the term "minimum-size standards." Up to this point, I had somehow managed to remain blissfully unaware of these codes; but, as the time for construction neared, my denial gave way to a grim reality. My proposed home was about one-third the size required to meet local limits. A drastic change of plans seemed unavoidable, but tripling the scale of a structure that had been designed to meet my specific needs so concisely seemed something like altering a tailored suit to fit like a potato sack.

I resolved to side-step the well-intentioned codes by putting my house on wheels. The construction of travel trailers is, after all, governed by maximum - not minimum size restrictions, and since Tumbleweed already fit within these, I had only to add some space for wheel wells to make the plan work.

At about eight by twelve feet plus a porch, loft, and four wheels, the resulting house

9

looked a bit like American Gothic meets the Winnebago Vectra. A steep, metal roof was supported by cedar-clad walls and turned cedar porch posts. The front gable was pierced by a lancet window. In the tradition of the formal plan, everything was symmetrical, with the door at exterior, front center. Inside, Knotty Pine walls and Douglas Fir flooring were contrasted by stainless steel hardware. There was a 7' x 7' great room, a closet-sized kitchen, an even smaller bathroom and a 3' 9"-tall bedroom upstairs. A cast-iron heater presided like an altar at the center of the space downstairs. In fact, the whole house looked a bit like a tiny cathedral on two, 3,500-pound axles.

The key to designing my happy home really was designing a happy life, and the key to that lay not so much in deciding what I needed as in recognizing all the things I can do without. What was left over read like a list I might make before packing my bags for a long trip. While I cannot remember the last time I packed my TV, stereo, or even the proverbial kitchen sink for any journey, I wanted this to be a list of items necessary not only to my survival, but to my contented survival. I am sure any hard-core minimalist would be as appalled by the length of my inventory as any materialist would be by its brevity. But then, I imagine nobody's list of necessities is ever going to quite match anybody else's. Each will read like some kind of self-portrait. I like to think that a house built true to the needs of its inhabitant will do the same.

Tumbleweed (facing page)

# Utilities

Like the rest of the house, utilities and appliances were designed with simplicity and sustainability in mind. They met my modest needs but would be considered primitive by conventional American standards. These rudimentary utilities certainly would not appeal to everyone interested in living in a small home, and it should be made clear that living small does not require deprivation. Hot and cold running water, a microwave oven, and cable TV are all available options.

Water: Tumbleweed was supplied by a simple, gravity-fed plumbing system. A two-and-a-half-gallon pot sat on a metal shelf just above a horizontal section of stovepipe in the overhead kitchen cabinet and drained into either the kitchen sink or shower through a Y intersection in a short stretch of rubber hose. The water was kept warm as long as the heat stove was on, and it could be made hot by setting the pot directly on the stove or a burner. The pot was filled at a nearby spigot. Gray water drained directly into the garden.

Heating and Cooking: The best source of heat most structures can use is that of the sun. I installed windows on all but what was intended as the north wall of Tumbleweed for good solar gain. A covered porch on the south side kept the heat of the high summer sun out while letting the lower winter rays flood the house with their warmth. A gas heater kicked in on cloudy days and cold nights. I chose a gas stove over a wood one mostly because gas stoves only require about one-sixth as much clearance from flammable surfaces. This, in turn, allowed me to have pine walls without having to put my heater right in the middle of an already tiny room. The cleanliness of gas also seemed to make sense in a small space, and I liked the idea of precise control with a thermostat rather than the frequent stoking that a small wood stove requires.

The propane tank that fed the heater also supplied an R.V. cooktop. It is upon this same double burner that a camp oven was set for baking.

Toilet: My composting toilet amounted to little more than an airtight bucket, a can of sawdust and a couple of compost piles outside. Sordid story short, the bucket was used as an indoor toilet and sawdust was put into the mix to absorb odor and balance out the carbon-to-nitrogen ratio. This bucket was emptied onto one compost pile or the other every so often, then rinsed. (Please see J.C. Jenkins, *The Humanure Handbook*, for details on this and other methods of composting human manure.) While the idea of carrying one's own poop (or anybody else's for that matter) to a compost pile off away from central living quarters may sound both inconvenient and plainly unacceptable to most Westerners, its appeal for more than a few will be its absolute efficiency. Without electricity, running water, or waste and only small inconvenience as its price, a cleaner environment and soil-building compost are made available.

Electricity: By now, these description of rudimentary plumbing and a plastic chamber pot may have made it sound as if my house was more derelict than homey. But, as I have said, these utilities were of my choice, and for me, choice is, in itself, a luxury. In fact, there was plenty of room for modern conveniences. The integral CD player, TV, and VCR disqualified the house as an ascetic's shanty. These appliances, along with six lights, two fans, and a radio, were all powered by the sun through a single solar panel. I chose not to mount the panel on my roof but kept it separate. This allowed me to situate the house in a shady place during the summer while collecting energy at the same time.

## Camping Out

I had managed to side-step building codes by constructing not a building, but a "travel trailer." With that stumbling block out of the way, I still faced a zoning problem. I wanted to live in town, and, like most towns, Iowa City does not allow trailer camping just anywhere. You cannot just buy an old lot and park there indefinitely. The restrictions do, however, allow for "camping out" in one's own backyard.

Upon discovering this, I snatched up a small fixer-upper on a large wooded parcel and proceeded to set up camp. The rent collected from the big house covered the ensuing mortgage and taxes. I would "camp out" in my own backyard for the next five years before selling the property and heading West.

## California

In 2005, I moved to the San Francisco Bay Area. I had heard a lot of horror stories about the price of properties in the region, so I sold Tumbleweed and built myself an even smaller house to take with me. I figured I had better have something I could parallel park, in case I had to live on the street for a while.

Tumbleweed's desk (left) and gas heater (above)

Tumbleweed's ladder (above), kitchen (opposite) and exteior (page 18)

XS exterior (page 19), loft (above)...

... and downstairs.

I called my next home XS-House (as in, "extra small"). It measured about 7' x 10'. Like Tumbleweed, it was on wheels, it had a steep metal roof, classic proportions and a pine interior punctuated by a metal heater on its central axis. A bathroom, kitchen, and sleeping loft featured essentially the same utilities as my previous residence. Unlike Tumbleweed, there was a four-foot long, stainless steel desk and a couch, and the exterior walls were clad in corrugated steel.

All things considered, my move westward went smoothly. Gale-force winds broadsided my tiny home all the way from Omaha to central Nevada, but both the house and the U-Haul came through unscathed.

I parked in front of the Sebastopol Whole Foods for three days. The U-Haul was almost due when a woman approached to ask if I would consider parking on her land to serve as a sort of groundskeeper. I would live just yards from a creek at the edge of a clearing in the redwoods. I would pay nothing and do nothing other than reside on the property. I was lodging amongst the redwoods by nightfall.

With my fear of having to live on the streets allayed, I built a new house and sold the XS before I had even settled in. I call my most recent domicile, "Tumbleweed 2." At 8' x 12' with a steep, metal roof over cedar walls, it looks just like the first Tumbleweed on the outside. I reconfigured the inside to accommodate a couple of additional puffy chairs and a five-foot long, stainless steel desk. I have been living in this house for nearly three years, and I have no intention of moving out any time soon (see pages 24 and 130 - 137 for photos).

## The Method and the Madness

My reasons for choosing to live in such small houses include some environmental concerns. The two largest of my three, hand-built homes were made with only about 4,800 pounds of building materials each, less than 100 pounds of which went to the local landfill. Each produced less than 900 pounds of greenhouse gases during a typical Iowa winter. And, at 89 square feet, plus porch and loft, each fit snugly into a single parking space.

In contrast, the average American house consumes about three quarters[1] of an acre of forest and produces about seven tons of construction waste. It emits 18 tons of greenhouse gases annually, and, at more than 2,349 square feet, it would most definitely not fit into a single parking space.

Finances informed my decision, too. Quality over quantity became my mantra. I have never been interested in building anything quite like a standard travel trailer or mobile home. Travel trailers are typically designed for more mobility and less year-round comfort than I like, while most manufactured housing looks too much like manufactured housing for my taste. Common practice in the industry (though not inherent or exclusive to it) is to build fast and cheap, then mask shoddiness with finishes. This strategy has allowed mobile homes to become what advocates call "the most house for your money." It has, in fact, helped to make manufactured housing one of the most affordable and, thus, most popular forms of housing in the United States today.

This is pretty much the opposite of the strategy I have adopted. I put the money saved on glitz and square footage into insulation, the reinforcement of structural elements, and detailing. At $30,000, Tumbleweed cost about one-sixth as much as the average American home. Only about $15,000 of this total was actually spent as cash on materials. That is less than half of what the average American household spends on furniture alone. The remaining $15,000 is about what I would have paid for labor had I not done it myself.

The cost of materials could have been nearly halved if more standard materials were used. A more frugal decision, for example, would have been to skip the $1,000, custom-built, lancet window and install a $100, factory-built, square one instead. But I was, and I remain, a sucker for beauty.

The total cost was low when you consider I was able to pay it off before I moved in—but not so low when you consider that I sunk over $300 into every square foot. The standard $110 per square foot might seem more reasonable, but I succumbed to the urge to invest some of the money saved on quantity into quality. As a result, my current residence is both one of the cheapest houses around and the most expensive per square foot.

Still, my main reason for living in such a little home is nothing so grandiose as saving the world, nor so pragmatic as saving money. Truth be told, I simply do not have the time or patience for a larger house. I have found that, like anything else that is superfluous, extra space merely gets in the way of my contentment. I wanted a place that would maintain my serene lifestyle, not a place that I would spend the rest of my life maintaining. I find nothing demanding about Tumbleweed. Everything is within arm's reach and nothing is in the way— not even space itself.

Tumbleweed 2 (above), Williamsburg, VA (next)

*Have nothing in your houses that you do not know to be useful, or believe to be beautiful.*
*- General George Pope Morris*

**PART TWO:**
**A GOOD HOME**

# A Good Home

A small house is not merely as good as its larger correlate; it is better. A home that is designed to meet its occupants' domestic needs for contented living without exceeding those needs will invariably surpass the quality of a bigger one in terms of sustainability, economics and aesthetics.

## Sustainability

Under no circumstances does a 3,000-square foot house for two qualify as "green." All the solar gain and reclaimed materials in the world can never change that. At 2,349 square feet, the average American house now emits more carbon dioxide than the average American car.[2]

Our houses are the biggest in the world—four times the international average. Since 1950, the median size of a new American house has more than doubled, even though the number of people per household shrank by more than 25 percent.[3] Not so long ago, you could expect to find just one bathroom in a house; but, by 1972, half of all new homes contained two or more bathrooms. Ten years later, three-quarters did. More bathrooms, more bedrooms and dens, bigger rooms overall, and, perhaps most notably, more stuff, have come to mean more square footage. America's houses have, quite literally, become bloated warehouses full of toys, furniture and decorations, and a lot of things we may never see or use.

As prodigal as this may seem already, even a space capable of meeting our extravagant living and storage needs is not always enough. We still have to worry about impressing a perceived audience. Entire rooms must be added to accommodate anticipated parties that may never be given and guests

The "American Dream"

who may never arrive. It is not uncommon for a living room to go unused for months between social gatherings and, even then, quickly empty out as guests gravitate toward the informality of the kitchen.

Until recently, the issue of over-consumption was conspicuously absent from mainstream green discourse. You are unlikely to find the answer to sprawl offered in a sustainable materials catalogue. Accountable consumption stands to serve no particular business interest. Building financiers and the real estate industry are certainly pleased with the current situation. Bigger is better, from their perspective, and they are always eager to tell us so.

If you do only one thing to make your new home more environmentally sound, make it small. Unless supporting the housing industry is the kind of sustainability you hope to achieve, a reasonably-scaled home is the best way there is to make a positive difference with real estate.

## Economics

"Economical" means doing only what is necessary to getting a job done. Anything more would be wasteful and contrary to the inherent simplicity of good design. An economical home affords what is essential to the comfort of its occupants without the added burden of unused space. Excess and economy are mutually exclusive. We can have exorbitance, or we can have the serenity that a sensibly-scaled home affords, but we cannot have both. Like anything else that is not essential to our happiness, extra space just gets in the way. It requires maintenance and heating, and ultimately demands that we exchange a portion of life for the money needed to pay for these extras.

For most Americans, big houses have come to symbolize the good life; but, all symbolism aside, the life these places actually foster is more typically one of drudgery. Mortgage payments can appropriate thirty to forty percent of a household's income not counting taxes, insurance, or maintenance expenses. When every spare penny is going towards house payments, there is nothing left over for investments, travel, continued education, more time with the kids, or even so much as a minute to relax and enjoy life. At this rate, an oversized house can start to look more like a debtor's prison than a home.

In 2008, a used house in the U.S. averaged about $244,000. That is far more than the average American can afford. Affordable housing has, in fact, become the exception. How seldom one hears of moderately-priced real estate

A cabin at The Whidbey Institute's Chinook Conference & Retreat Center (right)

referred to simply as "housing" and the pricier stuff as "unaffordable housing. "

The perception of affordable housing as something below par is not solely the result of this skewed terminology. The structures produced under the banner are usually as elephantine as the more expensive option, but with shoddier materials and even worse design. Through the eyes of the housing industry, square footage pays; quality does not.

Square footage is really the cheapest thing that can be added onto a house. The electrical system, plumbing, heating, appliances and structural components of most any dwelling are similar in at least one key way. They are all expensive. This costly core is housed by the relatively cheap volume that surrounds it.

In light of all this, it might seem that you really can't afford to buy anything less than the most house you can get your hands on. At first glance, it appears that the more you buy the more you save, but it's the hidden costs that get people into trouble. After all, more house than you need comes with more debt in total, more utility bills, more maintenance than you need and more foreclosures and more bailouts than any of us needs ever again.

Houses in Langly, WA, Bodega, CA and Mendocino, CA  (pages 29, 30 & 31, respectively)

Taos Pueblo (above) and a house on Highway 550 in New Mexico (right)

## Aesthetics

Today's market suggests that, for many of us, the perceived prestige of enormity takes precedence over design and even structural integrity when choosing a home. It seems that even a shoddy status symbol, with its expansive vinyl walls and snap-on plastic window grills, can somehow connote distinction. The finer qualities of design have become as difficult to market as they are to achieve, so they are being replaced by highly-prized square footage.

Just as something is typically appreciated as good or beautiful when it is deemed necessary, it will be condemned as ugly or evil when it is considered pointless. Under the right circumstances, murder becomes heroism and trash turns into treasure. The distinction between valuables and garbage is based primarily on our notions of utility. What two people see as beautiful will vary as much as what they consider to be useful.

Accordingly, the selfish squandering of valuable resources and the emission of toxins without *any* worthwhile purpose are always corrupt and unsightly. Beauty may be in the eye of the beholder, but an oversized house is an ugliness we all have to contend with.

A house in Bodega, CA

## Make Yourself At Home

A good dwelling offers more than shelter and security. A truly good house evokes a sense of home. Our sense of home comes from within us. It emerges when we enter an environment with which we can identify. This sense is not exclusive to one's own house. It can surface whenever we feel safe enough to be completely ourselves — beyond all insecurity and pretension.

A house founded on pretension and insecurity will seldom, if ever, make us feel anything more than pretentious and insecure. For a place to feel safe, it must first earn our trust. It must be honest, and an extra couple of thousand square feet tacked on in a vain attempt to conceal our insecurity is not honest.

Home is our defense against what can sometimes seem like a chaotic and demanding world. It is a fortress built from the things and principles that we value most. The inclusion of anything else is like a crack in the fortress wall. Order and tranquility are compromised when things that are extraneous to our happiness surround us. Unnecessary elements in the home dilute the intensity of the life within. Only when everything in our immediate environment is essential to our contented survival will home and the life within take on a truly essential quality.

Too many of our houses are not a refuge from chaos but merely extensions of it. The sense that our lives may not be entirely whole results in a desire for something more to fill the perceived void. This can lead to the purchase of an oversized house in which substance is obscured by excess. The happiness we really seek cannot be found by purchasing more space or more stuff. Those who do not recognize what is enough will never have enough.

Taos Pueblo

A Sausalito houseboat

# Too Good To Be Legal

It is illegal to inhabit a tiny home in most populated areas of the U.S. The housing industry and the banks sustaining it spent much of the 1970s and 1980s pushing for larger houses to produce more profit per structure, and housing authorities all cross the country adopted this bias in the form of minimum-size standards. The stated purpose of these codes is to preserve the high quality of living enjoyed in our urban and suburban areas by defining how small a house can be. They govern the size of every habitable room and details therein. By aiming to eliminate all but the most extravagant housing, size standards have effectively eliminated housing for everyone but the most affluent Americans.

## No Problem Too Small

Again, the intention of these limits is to keep unsightly little houses from popping up and lowering property values in America's communities and, moreover, to ensure that the housing industry is adequately sustained. The actual results of the limits are a greater number of unsightly large houses, inordinate construction waste, higher emissions, sprawl and deforestation, and, for those who cannot afford these larger houses, homelessness.

One of the leading causes of homelessness in this country is, in fact, our shortage of low-income housing. After mental illness and substance abuse, minimum-size standards have probably kept more people on the street than any other contributing factor. Countless attempts to design and build efficient

Another Sausalito Houseboat (above)

forms of shelter by and for the homeless have been thwarted by these codes. By demanding all or nothing from our homes, current restrictions ensure that the have-nots have nothing at all. The U.N. Declaration of Universal Human Rights (of which the United States is a signatory) holds shelter to be a fundamental human right. Yet, in the U.S.. this right is guaranteed only to those with enough money to afford the opulence.

The stated premise of these well-intentioned codes is as profoundly flawed as their results. Little houses have not been shown to lower the values of neighboring large residences. In fact, the opposite holds true. When standard-sized housing of standard materials and design goes up next to smaller, less expensive dwellings, for which some of the budget saved on square footage has been invested in quality materials and design, the value of the smaller places invariably plummets while that of the derelict mansions is raised.

Protecting "the health, safety and welfare not only of those persons utilizing a house but the general public as well" is the stated purpose of minimum-size standards. But, by prohibiting the construction of small homes, these codes clearly circumvent their own alleged goal. It would seem far more effective to outlaw the kind of toxic real estate that such codes currently mandate. An even more reasonable and less draconian system would allow individuals to determine the size of their own homes- large or small.

Some of us prefer to devote our time to our children, artistic endeavors, spiritual pursuits or relaxing. Others would rather spend their time generating disposable income. Some enjoy living simply, while others like taking risks. Every American should be free to choose a simple or an extravagant lifestyle and a house, to accommodate it.

## Mi Casa Es Su Asset

In his book, *How Buildings Learn*, Stuart Brand speaks of the difference between "use value" and "market value":

> Economists dating back to Aristotle make a distinction between "use value" and "market value." If you maximize use value, your home will steadily become more idiosyncratic and highly adapted over the years. Maximizing market value means becoming episodically more standard, stylish, and inspectable in order to meet the imagined desires of a potential buyer. Seeking to be anybody's house it becomes nobody's.[5]

On the surface, small dwellings may seem to afford greater utility than marketability. These places are typically produced by people who are more concerned about how well a house performs as a home than how much it could sell for. The creation of a smart little house has traditionally been a labor of love because, until recently, love of home has been its only apparent reward. As a rule, Americans like to buy big things. Like fast food, the standard American house offers more frills for less money. This is achieved primarily by reducing quality for quantity's sake.

Financiers have been banking on this knowledge for decades. From their perspective, a sound investment is one that corresponds with the dominant market trend. Oversized houses are more readily financed because they are what most Americans are looking for. For a lender, two bedrooms are better than one, because, whether the second room gets used or not, this is what the market calls for. Sometimes a bank will simply refuse to finance a small home because the cost per square foot is too high or the land upon which the house sits is too expensive in proportion to the structure. The design, construction or purchase of a small house has thus been further discouraged.

Despite all obstacles, a few relentless claustrophiles do continue to fight for their right to the tiny, and it has finally begun to pay off. Lawsuits concerning the constitutionality of minimum-size standards have recently forced some municipalities to drop the restrictions. Where this is the case, little dwellings have begun to pop up, and they are selling fast. Americans looking for smaller, well-built houses are out there, and their needs have been refused for decades. This minority, comprised mostly of singles, may be small, but it is ready to buy. It seems the composition of American households changed some time ago, and the dwellings that house them are just now being allowed to catch up.

Some developers on the West Coast have been quick to take advantage of the fresh market potential. In one high-income neighborhood, new houses of just 400 square feet are selling for over $120,000, and some at 800 square feet are going for more than $300,000. That is about 10 percent more per square foot than the cost of 2,000 square-foot houses in the immediate area. Needless to say, post-occupancy reports show that, though less expensive overall, these little homes have not had a negative impact on neighboring property values. In fact, the resale value of American houses of 2,500 square feet or more appreciated 57 percent between 1980 and 2000, while houses of 1,200 or less appreciated 78 percent (Elizabeth Rhodes, *Seattle Times*, 2001). Small houses appreciated $37 more per square foot.

## Meeting Code

I should be clear that, despite the absurdities in their codebooks, our local housing officials are not necessarily absurd people. This is important to remember if you are about to seek their approval for a project. Building codes are made at the national level, but they are adopted, tailored and enforced at the local level. View your housing department as the helpful resource it wants to be, not as an adversary. Once your local officials are politely informed about the actual consequences of the codes they have been touting, the codes are likely to change. Be sure to provide plenty of evidence about the merits of smaller houses, including documentation of projects similar to the one you intend to build. Codes are generally amended annually by means of a review and hearing process anyone in the community can take part in.

Diplomacy is one way of clearing the way for a small house. Moving is another. Some remote areas of the country have no building codes at all, and a few others have a special "owner-builder" zoning category that exempts people who want to build their own homes from all but minimal government oversight. Provisions for alternative construction projects also exist. Section 104.11 of the International Building Code encourages local departments to weigh the benefits of alternative design, materials and methods in the course of evaluating a project. Several counties permit accessory dwellings. These small outbuildings are also known as "granny flats" because they can be inhabited by a guest, teenager, or elderly member of the family.

Terminology can sometimes provide wiggle-room within the laws. "Temporary housing" is, for example, a term often used by codebooks to describe "any tent, trailer, motor home or other structure used for human shelter and designed to be transportable and not attached to the ground, to another structure or to any utility system on the same premises for more than 30 calendar days." Such structures are usually exempt from building codes. So, as long as a small home is built to be portable, with its own solar panel, composting toilet, and rain water collection system (or just unplugged once a month), it can sometimes be inhabited on the lot of an existing residence indefinitely.

Most municipalities are eager to endorse a socially-responsible project, but occasionally, a less savvy housing department will dig in its heels. When relocating to an area where smaller homes are legal is not an option, there may still be recourse. Political pressure can be applied on departments to great effect. While an official may have no trouble telling one individual that his plans for an affordable, high-quality, ecologically-sound home will not fly, the same official may have a great deal more trouble letting his objections be known publicly through the media. Newspeople love a good David-and-Goliath story as much as their audiences do.

As mentioned earlier, minimum-size standards have been found to be uncon-stitutional in several U.S. courts. If all else fails, a lawsuit against the local municipality remains a final option. This strategy, and any involving politi-cal pressure through the media, should be reserved only for circumstances where all other avenues have been explored and exhausted. Remember that ridiculous codes do not usually reflect the mind-set of those who have been asked to enforce them. Take it easy on your local officials and they will more than likely make things easy for you.

## Guerilla Housing

We are in the midst of a housing crisis. The Bureau of the Census has determined that more than forty percent of this country's families cannot afford to buy a house in the U.S. Over 1,500 square miles of rural land are lost to compulsory new housing each year. An immense portion of this will be used for nothing more than misguided exhibitionism. We clearly need to change our codes and financing structure and, most importantly, our current attitudes about house size.

Minimum-size standards are slowly eroding as common sense gradually makes its way back onto the housing scene. Where negotiation and political pressure have failed to eradicate antiquated codes, lawsuits have generally succeeded. But these measures all take more time, money and patience than many of us can muster. To make things worse, local covenants prohibiting small homes are being enacted more quickly than the old prohibitions can be dismantled. These restrictions are adopted by entire neighborhoods of people needlessly fearful for their property values and lifestyle.

The process of changing codes and minds is slow, and the situation is dire. As long as law ignores justice and reason, just and reasonable people will ignore the law. Thousands of Americans live outside the law by inhabiting houses too small to be legal. Some of them cannot afford a larger home, while others simply refuse to pay for and maintain unused, toxic space. These people are invariably good neighbors: they live quietly, in fear of someone's reporting them to the local building inspector.

Williamsburg, VA (facing page) and Klamath, CA (above)

# The Good, the Bad and the Sprawling

Over-consumption is reflected not only in the scale of our houses, but in the sizes of our yards and streets as well. Oversized lots on vast roads, miles from any worthwhile destination, have made the American suburb as inhospitable as it is vapid.

Like the design of our houses, the form of our neighborhoods is mandated by a long list of governmentally-imposed regulations that reflect our national taste for the enormous. In most U.S. cities it is currently illegal to build places like the older ones pictured in this book. Taos Pueblo, Elfreth's Alley, and Rue de Petit-Champlain all violate current U.S. zoning ordinances. Narrow, tree-lined streets with little shops and houses sitting at the sidewalk's edge are against the law. Countless state, federal and private bureaucracies work hard to uphold these restrictions. The Federal Housing Administration, the Department of Transportation, the auto, housing and oil industries and a host of others have a lot at stake in suburban sprawl and the policies that perpetuate it. Our government has been championing sprawl ever since the 1920s, when Secretary of Commerce, Herbert Hoover, persuaded realtors, builders, bankers, road-building interests and the auto industry to form a lobby that would push for increased development to boost the U.S. economy.

Essentially, zoning laws have been determining the form of our neighborhoods since the 1940s. Communities like the older ones pictured on these pages somehow managed without them. Since its inception, zoning has brought us immense, treeless streets, mandatory car ownership, and densities so low that the cost of infrastructures has become nothing short of exorbitant.

## Streets Too Wide

One of the most readily-apparent products of zoning is the wide, suburban street. Roadways built before zoning emerged typically have 9-foot wide travel lanes. Now, most are required to have lanes no less than 12 feet wide. This allows for what traffic engineers call "unimpeded flow," a term some critics have aptly interpreted as "speeding".

Safety concerns have played a no less significant role in the widening of America's streets. During the Cold War, AASHTO (the American Association of State Highway Transportation Officials), pushed hard for streets that would be big enough to facilitate evacuation and cleanup during and after a nuclear crisis. Fire departments, too, continue to demand broader streets to accommodate their increasingly large trucks. Streets today are often fifty feet across because standard code after the 1940s has required them to allow for two fire trucks passing in opposite directions at 50 miles per hour.

Sometimes it is not a street's width but its foliage that presents the problem. Departments of transportation routinely protest that trees [also referred to as FHOs (Fixed and Hazardous Objects)] should not line state roads. Now, certainly safety is important, but the high costs of wide, treeless roads (financial and otherwise) might warrant some kind of cost/benefit analysis. Fortunately, we have several. The most widely published is that of Peter Swift, whose eight-year study in Longmont, Colorado, compared traffic and fire injuries in areas served by narrow and wide streets. He found that, during this period, there were no deaths or injuries caused by fire, while there were 227 injuries and ten deaths resulting from car accidents. A significant number of these were related to street width. The study goes on to show that thirty-six foot-wide streets are about four times as dangerous as those that are twenty-four

feet across. According to Swift's abstract, "current street design standards are directly contributing to automobile accidents."

This study and others like it suggest that we should begin to consider the issue of public safety in a broader context. Fire hazards are only part of a much larger picture. The biggest threat to human life is not fire but the countless accidents caused by America's enormous roadways.

Suburbs did not grow out of any particular human need or evolve by trial and error as an improvement to preexisting types of urbanism. The 'burbs, as we know them, were invented shortly after World War Two as a means of dispersing urban population densities. This invention precluded virtually all lessons learned from the urban design of years past. Even the most universal principles of good planning, used successfully from 5000 B.C. Mesopotamia to 2005 A.D. Seaside, Florida, were ignored. Perhaps the most startling departure from tradition was the omission of contained outdoor space. Human beings have a predilection towards enclosure. We like places with discernible boundaries. To achieve this desired sense of enclosure, a street cannot be too wide. More specifically, its breadth should not far exceed the height of the buildings that flank it. A street that is more than twice as wide as its buildings are tall is unlikely to satisfy our inherent desire for orientation and shelter. Rows of trees can sometimes help to delineate a space and therebyincrease the recommended street-to-building ratio, but generally, anything wider than a proportion of 2:1 will compromise the quality of an urban environment.

America's suburbs incessantly ignore the 2:1 rule. The distance from a house to the one directly across the street is rarely less than five times the height of either structure, and there are seldom enough well-placed trees around to compensate. The empty landscape that results is one most of us have become far too familiar with.

To evoke a sense of place, a street, much like a dwelling, must be free of useless space. When given a choice, pedestrians will almost always choose to follow a narrow street instead of a wide one. That we frequently drive hours from our suburban homes to enjoy a tiny, lakeside cabin or the narrow streets of some old town is nearly as senseless as it is telling. That we then return to toil in our cavernous dwellings on deficient landscapes is more senseless, yet. The environments we see pictured in travel guides are typically the walkable, little streets of our older cities. The marketing agents who produce these guides are undoubtedly no less aware of our desire for contained, outdoor space than were the architects of the streets depicted.

People like places that were designed with people in mind, so it should come as no surprise that property values and street widths appear to share an inverse relationship. Apparently, we are willing to pay more for less pavement. The funny thing is that the skinny streets we like are actually much cheaper to build and maintain than the wide ones we so often choose to live with.

Quebec City

## Services Too Dispersed

Zoning as we know it basically began in nineteenth-century Europe. Industrialized cities were shrouded in coal smoke, so urban planners rightly suggested that factories be separated from residential areas. Life expectancies soared, the planners gloated, and segregation quickly became the new solution to every problem. So, while in the beginning only the incompatible functions of a town were kept apart, now everything is. Housing is separated from industry, low-density housing is kept separate from existing, higher-density housing, and all of this is kept far from restaurants, office buildings and shopping centers, which are all kept separate from each other.

With the dispersal have come mandatory car ownership and the end of pedestrian life as we once knew it. Where no worthwhile destinations can be easily reached on foot, there are no pedestrians, and where there are no pedestrians, there is no vitality.

This separation has simultaneously brought about an increase in the perceived need for ultra-autonomous houses. The idea that a house should contain everything its occupants could ever possibly need and then some is certainly not a new one, but it has achieved unprecedented popularity as houses have become increasingly remote from the services they traditionally relied upon. It now seems that every new residence must contain not only its own washer, dryer, dishwasher, high-speed internet access and big-screen home entertainment center, but enough kitchen, bathroom, dining and living space to serve as a nightclub for forty. The needs fulfilled by the corner grocery and local bar in our older neighborhoods are now assumed by 700 cubic-foot refrigerators and spacious, walk-in pantries. The resources currently required to support several million personal outposts cannot be sustained.

## Densities Too Low

Myths about high-density housing abound. It is widely believed, for example, that higher population densities necessarily increase congestion and strain infrastructures. This just simply is not the case. The congestion myth and the fear it inspires stem largely from some very real conditions that exist in our everyday world. Wherever a design does not accommodate for the number of people and the type of activities that occupy it, there will be overcrowding. But, just as with a house, the solution is not necessarily more space; it is usually better design.

The goal of design is the same for neighborhoods as it is for houses. Good community design has to meet our needs without far exceeding them. The suburbs fail on both these counts. People require open space; while the 'burbs do offer it on an excessive scale, the space is seldom useful. We inhabit outdoor space in specific ways, and the gaps left over between buildings and roads are seldom sufficient to accommodate our specific activities. The assumption that arbitrary swatches of pavement and bluegrass can well serve our outdoor requirements is mistaken. Such uninspired places rarely get used because they provide no sense of place or purpose.

High-density development is particularly conducive to comfortable outdoor environments. Providing enclosure without confinement is key. Consider architect Ross Chapin's Third Street Cottages in Langley, Washington. It is a "pocket neighborhood," comprised of eight, 975-square foot cottages and a shared workshop, all encircling a community garden. Eleven parking spaces have been provided out back. A footpath connects the houses and frames the common garden at center. A strong sense of enclosure is provided by the surrounding cottages and reinforced by a low, split-cedar fence separating the tiny private garden of each home from the shared one. This idyllic setting seems to hug without squeezing too hard. It is twice as dense as zoning normally allows for the area, and yet, there is not a trace of crowding.

Elfreth's Alley in Philadelphia offers another example of congestion-free, high-density development. The community was built before zoning laws were enacted. Elfreth's Alley was, in fact, established over 300 years ago and has been inhabited ever since. At about 20 feet wide with 25-foot-tall houses on either side, this development falls well within the parameters of the recommended building height-to-road width ratio. It is host to one-way automobile traffic, the residents of its 38 row houses, and thousands of tourists enjoying the all-too-rare experience of a place designed for people rather than cars. On this narrow, cobbled road flanked by brick, stone and foliage, it is easy to feel at home if only because it all makes perfect sense. There are no strange codes at work and no inexplicable abyss. It is not crowded, and it is not sparse. Like Third Street Cottages, Elfreth's Alley is exactly what it needs to be and nothing more. In each of these places, thoughtful design with particular attention to proportion and scale has been employed to make an environment where serenity and vitality coexist. Each should be a model for those designers and lawmakers who have a hand in our future.

Third Street Cottages on Whidbey Is.

Third Street Cottages on Whidbey Is.

Elfreth's Ally in Philadelphia

# Teaching By Example

Embracing less in a culture founded on the precept of more is counter-cultural, but it need not be self-consciously so. To do what we know to be right takes effort enough. There is no need to waste our much-needed energy on actively trying to change this spendthrift society. The tangible happiness of a life well lived is worth a thousand vehement protests.

Magazines, television and billboards incessantly insist that the cure for what ails us will be revealed by earning and spending more and increasing square footage. But the security and connectedness we seek are unobtainable so long as we continue to surround ourselves with these symbols of security and connectedness. Our desire for that which pretends to be success and our fear of not having it bar us from feeling genuinely fulfilled. Happiness lies in understanding what is truly necessary to our happiness and getting the rest out of the way.

Simplicity is the means to understanding our world and ourselves more clearly. We are reminded of this every time we pass by a modest little home. Occasionally, between the billboards, a tiny structure reveals a life that is unfettered by all of the excesses. Such uncomplicated dwellings serve to remind us of what we can be when our striving and fear are abandoned. Each person who chooses to live so simply inadvertently teaches the virtue of simplicity.

In a society as deeply mired in over-consumption as our own, embracing simplicity is more than merely countercultural; it can, at times, be downright scary. We are in many ways a herd animal, and to take the path less traveled requires courage. We are living in a system that, if left to its own devices, would have us in debt up to our eyeballs and still clamoring to purchase more things than we could use in a thousand lifetimes. Simplification requires that we consciously resist this system and replace it with a more viable one of our own making. For some of us, it requires that we either break laws or expend the time and money required to change those laws that currently prohibit an uncomplicated life.

In any case, anyone who sets out to create such a life should know that he or she is not alone. Though our current system discourages (even prohibits) such freedom, we are all, on some deeper level, familiar with our own need for simplicity. Order is a human concept that expresses an inherent human need. On at least the most intuitive level, we all see the beauty in a well-made, small dwelling because the necessity such a structure expresses resonates with the necessity within each of us. The fear that these little places sometimes inspire is not really so much one of lower property values; it is the fear that these simple dwellings may inadvertently tell us something important about ourselves that we are not ready to face.

Trinity Park, MA

Trinity Park, MA  (top) & a San Francisco Bungalow Court (above)

*You know you have perfection of design not when you have nothing more to add, but when you have nothing more to take away.*
-Antoine de Saint Exupery

# PART THREE: MAKING SPACE

# How to Build a House on Wheels

## The Foundation and Framing
With little exception, my first portable house was built by using the most standard methods of construction. Like any other mobile home, my structure sit on a steel chassis – in this case, a 7' x 14' flatbed, utility trailer. I took most of the wooden deck off to save weight and put aluminum flashing over the gaps to safeguard against mice. The floor framing was laid on top of that. I used two-by-fours spaced about 24 inches apart on center.

Once that framing was assembled, I filled the cavities between the boards with foam board insulation and spray foam and capped the whole thing off with some ¾-inch plywood subflooring.

The walls were framed right over the wheel wells using headers just as you would over any other opening. I used two-by-four studs and rafters spaced twenty-four inches on center rather than the more typical sixteen inches. This is a fairly standard practice used to save both money and natural resources. At this point, I was using it primarily to save weight. My flatbed was rated to hold 7,000 pounds.

## Bracing
Tumbleweed would have to withstand not only the normal wear and tear of everyday living, but also the occasional jolts and gale-force winds generated by highway travel. To prepare for this, I used what has come to be called the "screw-and-glue" method of sheathing. This means that a bead of construction adhesive was squeezed onto the entire length of every framing member

before 3/8" plywood sheathing was screwed (not nailed) to its surface. This makes for a structure far more resistant to lateral wind loads than sheathing secured with nails alone.

## Preventing Condensation

The only other special building consideration, after the foundation and bracing, for a little house on wheels is condensation. Unless they are insulated, sealed, and vented properly, small spaces are prone to a lot of condensation. It simply takes less time to fill the air in a small enclosure with the moisture caused by bathing, breathing, laundry, and cooking than it does to fill a large one. If that warm, moist air comes into contact with a sufficiently cold surface, it will condense into water. That is the reason that cars come equipped with defrosters, and that small houses need to be equipped with the right insulation, vapor retarders, and ventilation.

I used expanded polystyrene foam board as insulation with expanding spray foam in the seams for two basic reasons: 1) It takes a thicker piece of fiberglass batting to get the same amount of insulating power as you get out of a piece of extruded polystyrene. As I didn't have enough space for eight-inch-thick walls, this would have stood as reason enough for my choice. 2) Foam board is far more resistant to condensation.

With fiberglass batting and other porous insulations, you have to worry about moist air getting into it and condensing when the moisture gets to the cold part of the wall. At that point, the fluffy, pink stuff turns to mush, and mush doesn't insulate. It rots. To prevent this, you have to use a vapor retarder. This is usually just a large sheet of six-millimeter plastic hung over the inside surface of the batting and sealed at its edges. If your seals hold and your plastic does not rip, your fiberglass should stay fairly dry.

Expanded polystyrene with an impermeable coating does not need a vapor retarder. Being virtually waterproof makes it its own retarder. I chose the white, expanded polystyrene over the pink, extruded poly because, while I love the pink stuff for its superior insulating qualities, bugs love it, too.

The threat of condensation is also what prompted me to use double-glazed, insulated windows. The glass panes on a little abode can fog up pretty quickly unless they are well protected against the cold. I've found that windows sold with gas between the interior and exterior panes work pretty well for this purpose.

The other primary way to eliminate condensation in a small enclosure is by venting it. I installed a fan at the peak of my loft. It sucks moisture-laden air out of my living quarters when I am cooking or bathing and helps keep the place cool during the summer. On cold days, the vent can be sealed with a plug I cut from some leftover scraps of foam board.

## Tools

My tools are pictured on the facing page. They are pretty much all I have needed to build a dozen small houses. Folks I've worked with tell me I'm a fool for not using a table saw, too. You might want to add one to your list.

*1. skill saw, 2. jig saw, 3. plyers, 4. files, 5. miter saw, 6. hammer, 7. wrench, 8.goggles, 9. tape measure, 10. drill & drill bits, 11. pencil, 12. box cutter, 13. level, 14. chisel.*

1

2

3

4

5

6

7

8

9

10

11

12

13

14

## Step-By-Step Instructions

1) Buy your materials and order your windows. Be sure the trailer will accommodate the weight of your house. Cut any extra vertical parts off the trailer, but leave the wheel wells intact. Remove all the decking you can. Leave no more than 24" between the remaining boards. These gaps should be covered with aluminum flashing to guard against rodent and water infiltration. Do not put any beneath the porch.

2) Assemble the floor framing in front and in back of the wheel wells. Then connect the two sections by framing between the wells. Use screws instead of nails for this and all your framing.

3) Fill the cavities with your choice of insulation (in this case, expanded polystyrene foam board with expanding spray foam at the seams). Once again, the porch area should be left open to let water drain through it.

4) Once you cover the whole thing with 3/4" flooring or a subfloor, the exterior wall framing can be erected all along the perimeter. Connect the walls by driving screws through the bottom plates into the floor framing below.

5) Put up temporary, diagonal braces to steady the project while you work. Then install the collar beams (ceiling joists). The framing over the wheel wells is supported by horizontal headers which are, in turn, supported by the wheel wells.

6) Screw and glue CDX plywood to the exterior surface, and cut openings for the windows and door(s) with your skill saw.

7) Frame the roof and gables. Be sure to fasten the rafters to the walls with metal hurricane clips so that the entire roof does not blow off onto the highway.

8) Staple house-wrap to the walls. Go ahead and cut holes in the wrap if you anticipate dry weather or if your windows and door(s) are available for installation.

9) Waterproof the roof with tar paper or some equivalent. Then, run some 1/4" lath up the sides of the house. Place each over a stud. The channels between the strips will serve as air spaces to vent beneath the siding. This would also be a good time to trim the corners and openings and to put facia boards up around the eaves and rakes.

10) Use metal roofing if you plan on moving the house much. Asphalt shingles and most other materials are far more prone to blowing off. When the roof is done, you can put up your siding. Drive screws through it into the lath, and studs below. Caulk the seams where boards meet the wheel wells.

11) Fill the wall cavities with your insulation of choice, and frame the interior walls. Then, run the wires and pipes for your plumbing and electrical systems. I like to hire professionals to do most of the utilities, as these require a whole new skill set. If your insulation is water-permeable, this would be the time to hang some sort of vapor barrier to protect it from potential condensation problems.

12) Your interior wall finish can now be hung. I generally use thin, knotty pine tongue-and-groove paneling because it is so light and easy to install, but drywall and other materials will work, too, so long as you do not exceed your trailer's weight limit.

13) If your windows and doors are not in place by now, then this would be the time to insert them. You can also start building and/or installing any cabinetry and built-ins you intend to include.

14) Put your integral appliances in place and trim your edges. I do tend to put the screws aside and use nails and glue for this part. Finish work is, by far, the most time-consuming part of the entire building process, but, when it is done, your house is done, too. Make yourself at home.

The finished product (right)

# Subtractive Design

A well-designed little house is like an oversized house with the unusable parts removed. Such refinement is achieved through subtractive design — the systematic elimination of all that does not contribute to the intended function of a composition. In the case of residential architecture, everything not enhancing the quality of life within a dwelling must go. Anything not working to this end works against it. Extra bathrooms, bedrooms, gables and extra space require extra money, time and energy from the occupant(s). Superfluous luxury items are a burden. A simple home, unfettered by extraneous gadgets, is the most effective labor-saving device there is.

Subtractive design is used in disciplines ranging from industrial design to civil engineering. In machine design, its primary purpose is demonstrated with particular clarity. The more parts there are in a piece of machinery, the more inefficient it will be. This is no less true of a home than it is of an engine.

## Remembering Common Sense

Most of our new houses are really not designed at all, but assembled without much thought for their ultimate composition. Architects seldom have anything to do with the process. Instead, a team of marketing engineers comes up with a product that will bring in more money at less cost to the developer. The team's job is to devise a cheap structure that people will actually pay good money for. Low-grade, vinyl siding, ornamental gables and asphalt shingles have become their preferred medium. Adding extra square footage is about the cheapest, easiest way there is to increase a property's market value, so it is applied liberally without any apparent attempt to make the additional space particularly useful. The final product is almost always a bulky conglomeration of parts without cohesion — a success, by industry standards, where over-sized invariably equals big profits.

Even when left to certified architects, the design of our homes can some-times be less than sensible. Too frequently, a licensed architect's self-per-ceived need for originality takes precedence over the real needs of his or her clients. Common sense is abandoned for frivolous displays of talent. Where a straight gable would make the most sense, a less savvy architect will throw in a few cantilevers and an extra dormer, just for show. Subtractive design is abandoned for hopes of personal recognition and for what is likely to be a very leaky house. Common sense is an inherent part of all great architecture. Sadly, this crucial resource has become anything but common in the creation of residential America.

Certainly the most famous example of those whose aspirations for a good name took precedence over good design was Frank Lloyd Wright. Wright was fond of innovative methods and extravagant forms. Those novel houses that once earned him recognition as a peerless innovator have since earned him another kind of reputation. Leaks are a part of many Wright houses. Wright has become infamous not only for his abundant drips but for his im-pudent dismissal of their significance. "If the roof doesn't leak," he professed, "the architect hasn't been creative enough." And to those clients who dared to complain about seepage, he would repeatedly quip, "That's how you can tell it's a roof."

Subtractive design is integral to, and nearly synonymous with, vernacular design. Both entail planning a home that will satisfy its inhabitants' domestic needs without far exceeding them. This is also what is known as common sense. When applied to buildings, the word "vernacular" in fact means "common": that is to say "ordinary" and "of the people." In contrast to housing that is made by professionals for profit or fame, vernacular housing is designed by ordinary folks simply striving to house themselves by the most proven and effective means available.

Webster's defines *vernacular* as "architectural expression employing the commonest forms, materials, and decorations" (*Webster's Third New International Dictionary,* G. and C. Merriam Co. 1966. p. 2544). If a particular type of roof works better than any other, then that is what is used. In short, vernacular architecture is not the product of invention, but of evolution—its parts plucked from the great global stew pot of common knowledge and common forms. Anything is fair game so long as it has been empirically proven to work well and withstand the test of time. By using only tried-and-true forms and building practices, such design successfully avoids the multitude of post-occupancy problems typical of more "innovative" architecture.

The vernacular home does not preclude modern conveniences. There are, after all, better ways to insulate these days than with buffalo skins. The vernacular designer appropriates the best means currently available to meet human needs, but, technology is, of course, employed only where it will enhance the quality of life within a dwelling and not cause undue burden.

Mendocino gable (right)

## All Natural

What the subtractive process requires, more than anything else, is a firm understanding of necessity. Knowledge of universal human needs and the archetypal forms that satisfy them is a prerequisite for the practice of good design. This knowledge is available to anyone willing to pay attention.

A vernacular architect who has come across a photo of a Kirghizian yurt and encountered a Japanese unitized bathroom and a termite mound while traveling does not set out to build a yurt with a unitized bathroom and termite inspired air conditioning just to show what he has learned. He retains the forms for a time when necessity demands their use.

Vernacular architects do not strive to produce novel designs for novelty's sake. Necessity must be allowed to dictate form. The architect's primary job is to get out of its way. It might seem that such a process would produce a monotonously limited variety of structures, but, in fact, there is infinite variation within the discipline. Vernacular architecture is as diverse as the climates and cultures that produce it. The buildings in a particular region may all look similar as they have all resulted from the same set of socionatural conditions, but within these boundaries, there is also plenty of room for variance. With the big problems of design already resolved by the common sense of their predecessors, vernacular architects are left free to focus on the specifics of the project at hand. Instead of reinventing the wheel, they are left to fine-tune the spokes.

## Symbolic Meaning

Vernacular architects have at their disposal not only what they have assimilated from books, travel and the work of their ancestors but a lot of hard-wired knowledge as well. Human beings have an innate understanding of certain forms. We are born liking some shapes more than others, and our favorites turn up frequently in the art of young children and in every culture. Among these is the icon representing our collective idea of home. Everyone will undoubtedly recognize the depiction of a structure with a pitched roof, a chimney accompanied by a curlicue of smoke and a door flanked by mullioned windows. Children draw this as repeatedly and as spontaneously as they do faces and animals. It represents our shared idea of home, and, not suprisingly, it includes some of the most essential parts of an effective house. With little exception, a pitched roof to deflect the elements, with a well-marked entrance leading into a warm interior, with a view to the world outside are exactly what are necessary to a freestanding home. For a vernacular designer, any deviation from this ideal is dictated by the particular needs posed by local climate.

The symbolic meaning of common architectural shapes is as universal as the use of the shapes themselves. Just as surely as we look for meaning in our everyday world, the most common things in our world do become meaningful. That the symbolism behind these objects is virtually the same from culture to culture may say something about the nature of our less corporal desires. It seems necessary that we see ourselves as part of an undivided universe. Through science, religion, and art, we strive to make this connection. On an intuitive level, home reminds us that the self and its environment are inextricable. Archetypes like the pierced gable are not contrived, but rather turn up naturally wherever necessity is allowed to dictate form and its content.

Mac Callum House in Mendocino ,CA

It just so happens that the most practical shapes are also the most symbolically loaded. Those forms best-suited to our physical needs have come to hold special meaning for us. The standard gabled roof not only represents our most primal idea of shelter, but also embodies the most universal of all abstract concepts, that of All-as-One. This theme has been the foundation for virtually every religion and government in history, and there may very well be an illustration of it in your purse or wallet at this very moment.

The image of the pyramid on the back of the U.S. dollar represents the four sides of the universe (All) culminating at their apex as the eye of God (One). The phrase "E Pluribus Unum" (from many, one) appears elsewhere on the bill along with no less than three other references to the archetype.

The common gable with a window at its center is vernacular architecture's one-eyed pyramid. The duality of its two sides converging at their singular peak represents divinity, and is again underscored by a single central window. All of this rests on four walls, which are universally symbolic of the cosmos.

Tumbleweed Tiny House Company's Epu with the wheels removed.

# Form and Number

The meaning of numbers and shapes is as universal as the use of the shapes themselves. Those that turn up in nature most often, like circles, squares, 1, 1.6, 2, 3, 4, 12 and 28 tend to be the most symbolically loaded.

*One* is a single point without dimension, typically represented by the circle created when a line is drawn around the point with a compass. One symbolizes the divine through its singularity.

*Two* adds dimension through the addition of a second point. It is commonly depicted by the Vesica Piscis shape that occurs when two circles overlap. It represents duality and creativity.

*Three* brings balance back to two. It is represented by the triangle and symbolizes variations on the Trinity.

*Four,* as embodied by the square, typically represents the world we live in, with its four cardinal directions.

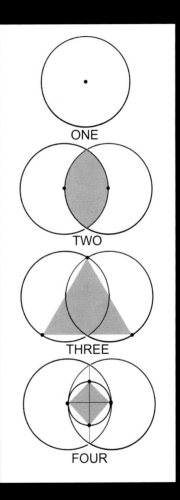

ONE

TWO

THREE

FOUR

# Organizing Principles

The success of a work of art hinges, more than anything else, on the strength of its composition. Here the term "composition" is used to mean "a whole comprised of parts." A strong composition is one in which all its parts work to strengthen the whole. This is as true of a piece of music as it is of a painting or the design of a small house.

The last chapter described subtractive design as the means to distilling a house to its essential components. This chapter will focus primarily on how the remaining parts are to be organized into a comprehensive whole. Seven principles: simplicity, honesty, proportion, scale, alignment, hierarchy and procession will be presented as essential considerations to meeting this end.

## Simplicity

It is ironic that simplicity is by far the most difficult of the seven principles to achieve. Simplification is a complicated process. It demands that every proportion and axis be painstakingly honed and that every remaining detail be absolutely essential. The more simplified a design becomes; the more any imperfection is going to stand out. Everything in a plain design must make sense, because every little thing means so much. The result of this arduous effort will look like something a child could come up with. The most refined art always looks as if it had been easy to achieve.

This sort of streamlining demands a firm understanding of what is necessary to a home. As stated before, there is no room in an honest dwelling for anything apart from what truly makes its occupant(s) happy. Each one of us must ultimately decide what this is and is not for ourselves. But, as with all good vernacular processes, we should first consider the findings of those who have gone before us. While our domestic needs will differ as much as our location and circumstances, a look at what others consider to be important can get us going in the right direction.

Ideas about what is indispensable to a home can be concise so long as they are kept abstract. Consider Cicero's claim: "If you have a garden and a library, you have everything you need." And William Morris' sage advice: "Have nothing in your houses that you do not know to be useful, or believe to be beautiful." More pragmatic lists tend to be a bit longer. Small house advocate, Ron Konzak, is helpful. In his essay, entitled: "Prohousing," Konzak explains that most every domicile should provide...

1. Shelter from the elements.
2. Personal security.
3. Space for the preparation and consumption of food.
4. Provision for personal hygiene.
5. Sanitary facilities for relieving oneself.
6. Secure storage for one's possessions.

In their now-famous book, *A Pattern Language*, Christopher Alexander and his colleagues provide a detailed list of no fewer than 150 items for possible inclusion in a home. I have made a similar, albeit far less detailed, list here. More asterisks indicate a more universal need for the item they accompany.

EXTERIOR:
1. A small parking area out back.
2. A front door that is easily identified from the street.****
3. A small awning over the door to keep occupants dry as they dig for keys and guests dry as they wait for occupants.**

89

4. A bench next to the front door on which occupants can set things while fumbling for keys or sit while putting on/off shoes.
5. A window in the front door.
6. A steeply-pitched roof to better deflect the elements.*
7. Adequate insulation in all doors, windows, walls, the floor and the roof.****
8. Windows on at least two sides of every room for cross ventilation and diffuse, natural light.
9. Windows on the front of the house.**
10. A structure for bulk storage out back.
11. A light over the front door.
12. No less than 10 square feet of window glass for every 300 cubic feet of interior space.**
13. Eaves

ENTRY:
14. A light switch right inside the front door.*
15. A bench just inside the front door on which occupants can set things while fumbling for keys or sit while putting on/off shoes.
16. A closet or hooks near the door for coats, hats and gloves.*

A PLACE TO SIT:
17. A chair or floor pillow for each member of the household.****
18. Some extra chairs or pillows for guests. (In bulk storage?)*
19. A table for eating, with a light overhead.**
20. A table for working, with a light overhead.**
21. Nearby shelves or cabinets for books, eating utensils or anything else pertinent to the activity area.
22. A private place for each member of the household.***

23. A phone.

A PLACE TO LIE DOWN:
24. A bed.***
25. A light at or above the head of the bed.
26. A surface near the head of the bed on which to set a clock, tissue, books, etc.

APPLIANCES AND UTILITIES:
27. Electricity and a place for the accompanying fuse box.**
28. A source of water and sufficient room for water pipes.***
29. A water heater.**
30. A source of heat.**
31. A place for an air conditioner.
32. Ventilation and room for any accompanying ductwork (windows can sometimes work to this end).****
33. An indoor toilet.*
34. A tub or shower.***
35. A towel rack near the tub or shower.**
36. A mirror.**
37. A home entertainment center.
38. A washer/dryer.

A PLACE TO COOK:
39. An appropriately-sized refrigerator.
40. A stove top.*
41. An oven.
42. A sink.***

43. A work surface for food preparation with a light over it.**
44. Shelves or cabinets near the work surface for food and cooking supplies.**

ADDITIONAL BULK STORAGE:
45. A laundry bin.
46. No less than 100 cubic feet of storage per occupant for clothes, books and personal items.****

These items are not mutually exclusive. Where one can serve two or more purposes, so much the better. The dining table, for example, may double as a desk. This is especially true in a one-person household, where a single piece of furniture will rarely be used for more than one purpose at a time. Also, keep in mind that many of these things can be tucked away while not in use.

This list is meant to be a starting place from which anyone can begin to decide what is necessary to their own home. Certainly, what I propose to be universal requirements will not be universally agreed upon. The only needs that really matter in the design of a home are those of its occupant(s). The important thing to keep in mind when creating one's own list is that the less significant a part is to the whole and its function, the more it will diminish the quality of the overall design. Just remember when to say "when."

# Honesty

In the most beautiful houses, no attempt is made to conceal structural elements or disguise materials. Because wooden collar beams are understood as necessary, they are also seen as beautiful. Whenever possible, features like these are left unpainted and exposed to view. Then there are those houses for which attempts are made to mimic the solid structure and materials of more substantial homes. These are easily recognized by their wood-grain textured, aluminum siding, hollow vinyl columns and false gables.

Aluminum is a fine material so long as it is used as needed and allowed to look like aluminum. Artifice is artless. It does not merely violate nature's law of necessity, but openly mocks it. If wood is required for a job, wood should be used and allowed to speak for itself. If aluminum is required, aluminum should be used and its beauty left ungilded whenever possible.

Ornamental gables are to a house what the comb-over is to a head of hair. The vast disparity between the intention and result of these two contrivances is more than a little ironic. Both are intended to convince us that the homeowner (or hair owner, as the case may be) feels secure in his position, but as artifice, each only serves to reveal insecurity and dishonesty.

False gables are tacked onto the front side of a property in a vain attempt to prove to us that the house is spectacular. While this effort is not fooling anybody, it is effectively serving to weaken the structural integrity of the roof. The more parts there are in a design, the more things can go wrong. Leaks almost never spring on a straight-gabled roof, but in the valleys between gables, they are relatively common. Unnecessary gables compromise simplicity for what is bound to be a very expensive spectacle.

## Proportion

If these principles are starting to seem a lot like common sense, it is because they are. It is in our nature to seek out the sort of order that they prescribe. Honest structure and simple forms strike a chord with us because they are true to nature's law of necessity. Sound proportions strike a chord, too. Certain proportions seem to appear everywhere — in sea shells, trees, geodes, cell structure, and all of what is commonly called "the natural world." That these same proportions continually turn up in our own creations should not seem too surprising or coincidental. We are nature, after all, and so our works are bound to contain these natural proportions.

Proportioning is one of the primary means by which a building can be made readable. Repeated architectural forms and the spaces between them are like music, the pattern (or rhythm) of which we understand because it is always with us. We intuitively understand good proportions because they are a part of our most primal language.

On the most conscious level, good proportion is achieved by first choosing an increment of measure. Making such a seemingly arbitrary decision can be made easier if meaning is imposed on it. Ancient civilizations created systems of measure based on human and geodetic significance. A Mediterranian precursor to the foot we use today was 1/360,000 of 1/360 (one degree) of the circumference of the earth. It was also related to the conventional calendar containing 360 days of the year plus five holy days, and it was 1/6 the height of what were viewed as ideal human proportions. The eighteen-inch cubit (distance from elbow to longest finger tip) and the yard (1/2 of the total height) also relate to this canon. We have inherited a measuring system imbued with meaning that relates us to our environment. Our buildings are literally designed to embody the characteristics of the Self.

Today, plywood is milled to 4' x 8' pieces; lumber comes in 6', 8', 10', 12' and 16' lengths; metal roofing is typically 3' wide, and most other building materials are similarly sized to fit within this one foot system of measure. Great efficiency can be achieved by keeping this in mind during the design process. A large share of bragging rights deservedly go to a designer whose structure has left little construction waste and has required relatively few saw cuts. Simplified construction is nearly as much the aim of subtractive design as simplified form and function are.

The unit of measure we use to compose a harmonious design can be more than just linear. In Japan, a two-dimensional increment called the "tatami mat" is often used. It is an area of three by six feet (the Japanese foot, or *shaku*, is actually 11.93 of our inches). This area is meant to correlate with human dimensions. The Japanese saying, "tatte hanjo, nete ichijo," translates as, "half a mat to stand, one mat to sleep."

Once an increment has been chosen, be it a foot, yard, cubit, tatami mat or a sheet of plywood, we can begin to compose a home comprised of simple multiples and fractions of the unit. This process should be fairly intuitive. Each one of us will compose somewhat differently, but our underlying principles are the same. These principles are not arbitrary, but the same that govern the composition of all natural things.

Dee Williams' shouse in Olympia, WA

# Scale

*Always design a thing by considering it in its next larger context—a chair in a room, a room in a house, a house in an environment.* –Eliel Saarinen

Again, the scale of our homes should be determined by the true needs of their occupant(s). Few of us would go into a restaurant and seek out a table in the large, open space at the center of the dining room. Most of us prefer the comfort and security of the corner booth. Ideally, every room in our homes will offer the same sense of enclosure without confinement.

To be sure that a minimized space does not feel confining, its designer has to consider ergonomics and any pertinent anthropometric data. Understanding exactly how much space we occupy when we sit, stand or lie down is absolutely essential to the subtractive process. To know how much can be excised from our homes, we must first understand how much is needed. An extensive list of recommended dimensions is provided on pages 117 - 122. When a home's designer is also to be its sole inhabitant, a more personalized list can be made. Every measurement within a house, from the size of its doorways to the height of its kitchen counter, should ideally be determined by what feels good to the occupant. Designing one's own little house is more like tailoring a suit than what is normally thought of as architecture.

The overall scale of our homes does not need to accommodate every possible activity under the sun. With little exception, home is the place we go to sit and to lie around at the end of each day. There will also most likely be some cooking, eating, hygiene, working and playing going on, but none of these activities needs to occupy a palace. Remember, "half a mat to stand, one mat to sleep."

## Alignment

Gestalt psychologists have shown that compositions with long, continuous lines make more sense to us than those with a lot of little broken ones. Continuity allows us to read a composition as a whole. The principle of alignment is just one part of what some psychologists have termed the "simplicity" concept. This states that simple patterns are easier for us to comprehend than complex ones. This will come as no surprise to vernacular architects, who have been putting the concept to work for quite some time now. Common sense has always been the folk designer's greatest asset.

Alignment entails arranging the elements of a design along a single axis or arc whenever possible. When a group of columns is required, a savvy designer will not just put one over here and arbitrarily plop the next two down wherever chance or ego dictates. The designer will line them up in a row. The geometry of alignment may contain some real lines, like the kind produced by a solid wall, and it may have some implied ones, like the axis that runs through a row of well-ordered columns.

## Hierarchy

Good home design entails a lot of categorizing. The categories we use are determined by function. In organizing a home, everything that is used to prepare food would, for example, most likely go into the "kitchen" category. If something in the kitchen category functions primarily to wash dishes, it would probably be placed into the subcategory of "kitchen sink area." The categories proposed by our predecessors usually serve as pretty good tools for organizing a home. Ideas like "kitchen," "bathroom," and "bedroom" stick around because they generally work. But these ideas cannot be allowed to dictate the ultimate form of a dwelling; that is for necessity alone to decide.

# Sacred Geometry

Organizing the tops of windows and doors along a horizontal axis and deliberately spacing porch posts in a row are examples of the ways alignment and proportion can be consciously used to create a structure that makes visual sense. Less obvious examples become apparent when regulating lines are drawn on photos of a building's facade. These lines are stretched between significant elements, like from the peak of the roof to the cornerstones, or from a keystone to the baseplates. When geometry has been allowed to dictate the rest of the design, the lines will almost invariably intersect or align with other crucial parts of the building. The intersections are often unexpected, their appearance the unintended by-product of the creative process described on these pages

Do not think that, just because our shared idea of "bathroom" includes a bath, a sink and a toilet, that these things must always be grouped together behind the same door. The needs of a particular household may determine that each be kept separate so that more than one can be used at a time. What is more, if the kitchen sink is just outside the door to the toilet, then a separate basin may not be necessary at all. The distinctions made between the categories of "living room," "family room" and "dining room" might well be combined into the single category of "great room" for further consolidation.

Vernacular designers do not thoughtlessly mimic the form of other buildings. They pay close attention to them, use what works in their area, and improve upon what does not.

Along with all the categorizing that goes on during the design process, there is a lot of prioritizing that has to be done as well. The relative importance of a room and the things in it can be underscored by size and placement. The most important room in a small house, in both the practical and the symbolic sense, is almost always the great room or its farmhouse kitchen equivalent. To make its importance all the more clear, this area should occupy the largest share of the home and should be prominently located. In a small dwelling, it is generally best to position this space near the home's center, so that smaller, less significant rooms can be arranged around its periphery as alcoves.

Arranging the rooms and objects in a house according to their relative importance is essential to making any space readable. Presenting such a hierarchy may require that some doorways be enlarged to exaggerate one room's significance, or that a ceiling be lowered to downplay another's. As always, necessity will determine these things inasmuch as it is allowed to.

# Procession

While the principle of procession is still primarily about space, it also pertains to time. The best houses speak to us in a visual language with which we are all familiar. A gate in a picket fence that opens onto a narrow path that leads through a yard to an open porch that covers a door is a set of symbols we recognize as signposts guiding us through increasingly private territory towards the threshold of someone's clandestine world. Such "layering" (as it is often called) demarcates public space from semiprivate and private spaces. This serves to put us at ease, as it ensures that we will never be left to wonder if we have overstepped our boundaries as guests. Familiar symbols of domesticity, like the gable, can further comfort us by presenting the subconscious with the familiar language of home. A covered doorway that is clearly visible from the street not only lets us know where to enter a house, but indicates that we are welcome there. Generally, more private areas, like bedrooms and bathrooms, will be positioned towards the rear of a house and encountered only after more public realms, like the living room, have been passed.

Once inside a good dwelling, visual cues should leave us with no doubt that this is a home in the truest sense of the word. Some of the greatest residential designs employ the same formal geometry as that of sacred architecture. When we approach and enter a well-designed church or mosque, we immediately find ourselves straddling its vertical symmetry. As we follow the axis between our eye and the cross or qibla at the far end of the room, we remain at the building's center. This procession alludes to the structure's significance as a symbol of the cosmos of which we are the center. A well-designed little house will remind us just as effectively as any cathedral that we are not merely witnessing divine beauty, but that we are that beauty.

A strong procession is created in the home by using some variation of the same three elements that are universally used to create it in sacred architecture: a gate, a path and a focal point. Moreover, all seven of the principles that have been presented here for residential design are none other than the same used to design a good cathedral. Attention to simplicity, honesty, proportion, scale, alignment, hierarchy and procession can help to produce a composition in which we participate as an indispensable component. So long as the prescriptions for good design are followed, even the tiniest hut will never seem twee or out of place. A well-composed, little house reflects the entire universe as no ordinary mansion can.

Third Street Cottages in Langley, WA

# Execution

So far, this chapter has described the sensibility, the principles, and the tools inherent to successful architecture. This next section explains the actual process of subtractive design and relevant considerations. Compared to what is involved in producing large houses, planning a little home is relatively challenging. As stated earlier, a smart, little dwelling is just like an oversized house with the unnecessary parts removed. Editing a structure down to its essence takes patience, but so long as one has this and abides by these instructions as well as necessity, the effort will not go unrewarded.

***Get the right tools.*** There are as many techniques for putting architectural ideas down on paper (or screen) as there are people putting them down there. The best way I have found is with a .05 mm technical pencil, a Tuff Stuff retractable eraser, an 8 1/2" x 11" pad of 1/8" grid paper, a transparent ruler and a simple compass for making arcs. I know there are a lot of people out there who will swear by computer programs like CAD. My own experience with such programs is that they are great for tidying up finished designs but are no match for pencil and paper when it comes to the creative part of the process. Fluidity is essential, in any case.

***Keep the process fluid.*** Writer's block is not exclusive to writers. It can happen to any artist who forgets to keep an eye on the big picture. Because a successful composition is only possible when every one of its parts is integral to the whole, it makes sense that the whole must be more or less established before any part can be fully developed. The whole informs the shape and function of its parts. Work from the most general elements of the composition toward the more specific details within.

Do not consider anything too precious for revision until a composition has been established, the house has been proven to work perfectly. Expect to go through more eraser than graphite. Every mistake is a step forward, as it further illuminates what is not necessary and, thus, points the way to what is. Ninety percent of the process will be messy and temporal. Clean lines will only be introduced once the real work has been done.

**Know what is needed.** The process begins with general considerations and broad forms. Before proceeding, a list of domestic necessities, like the one provided on pages 89 - 92, should be developed according to the inhabitant's needs and those posed by the local environment.

**Determine the shape of the house**. Spherical forms have the least amount of surface area, so a dome is bound to need a bit less heating and cooling than something with square corners. On the other hand, domes are prone to leaks and are far more difficult to compose than rectilinear shapes. Right-angled forms invariably mesh with other right-angled forms, so books fit easily onto shelves, shelves into corners, corners into rooms, rooms into houses, houses into lots and lots into communities.

Buildings with flat roofs have become quite popular over the past century or so. The trend began in Europe, where elaborate roofs with lots of ornaments had become symbolic of the ruling class. Modernism stepped in to provide homeowners with the exact opposite of the ornate option. Flat roofs represented the more respectable, utilitarian lifestyle of the proletariat. Once Modernism hit America, it became the perfect excuse for putting up a lot of cheap buildings. Aside from adding unnecessary square footage, about the easiest way for builders to make more money for less is by sticking a flat roof on their structures.

Flat roofs may be all well and good when used in the most arid deserts of the U.S., but when used elsewhere, they tend to spring a lot of leaks or collapse. In such cases, the complexities of simplification become all too clear. By all means, that which is unnecessary to a design should be eliminated, but only after what is necessary has been determined.

Just as bees build with hexagons and cubitermes termites go for domes, we, as a species, tend to produce a lot of 90-degree angle walls and pitched roofs. It just seems to make sense for us. Rain and snow are a part of most of the climates we live in, and a slanted roof sheds these elements like nothing else can. Of course, flat roofs and domes are exactly what are needed in some situations, and, as always, necessity should be heeded.

***Determine the approximate size.*** I know people who live in just seventy square feet. I know other folks for whom living in anything less than ten times that might be difficult. Houses are not a one-size-fits-all product.

Lists detailing the amount of space needed for appliances and elbow room, as well as wall, floor and ceiling thickness are provided at the end of this chapter. Reference these as you proceed to determine and organize special needs.

If this is to be a place for yourself, you will have to figure out how much physical space is required for all of your things, for yourself, for other occupants and their stuff, and for guests. Remember that, with all of the money that will be saved by building a smaller dwelling, outsourcing hotel ball rooms for big parties will now be a viable way to extend your home beyond the limitations of the house itself. Your little abode should not be thought of as an autonomous structure, but more as the most private realm within a much broader system.

Calculating how much space is needed for your stuff is a pretty straightforward task. First, get rid of anything you do not need. Then, round up all your possessions and a measuring tape. Consider how many of the things will require closet space, how many will go on book shelves, in the kitchen, near the kitchen sink, and so on. Then proceed to determine how much open space you need for your own comfort. You will probably want one relatively-large, main room. To determine its size, find a smallish enclosure that is fairly uncluttered. Does it feel like a comfortable amount of space? How tall does it need to be? Consider what kind of activities you will be doing in your main room. If you anticipate some yoga, determine how large an area that requires. Office cubicles, bathroom stalls and walk-in closets are some places you might consider evaluating. Never mind the puzzled looks you will undoubtedly receive from others

**Sketch your rooms.** Once you have an idea of how much open area you require, draw a bird's-eye view of the main room on a piece of grid paper. Be sure to add some square footage around the edges for furnishings and storage. To keep its center unobstructed, most of the furniture will need to be kept on the periphery, along with some empty space for accessing windows and doors.

Detailed calculations should be saved for later. For now, just continue to cat-

categorize your things into areas and make to-scale drawings of any other rooms you plan to include. Keep the center of these spaces open too.

Cut the drawing of each room out and place all of them together as you imagine them fitting together in a house. If they do not add up to a simple, Euclidian shape, like a square, circle, rectangle or triangle, you may want to adjust their proportions until they do. Generally, the more corners there are on the outside of a house, the more surface area there will be to lose heat and A.C., the more materials and labor will be required, and the more complex and potentially leaky the roof will be. Four or five exterior corners are usually plenty. Anything with more than ten or so may become problematic. Alignment is particularly important for the outside of the house. Four, unbroken walls are generally better than a bunch of divided ones.

**Consider portals.** Decide how the rooms will be connected by doors and how the house will be connected to the outside world by windows and door(s). Think about how the placement of doors and windows will make the home's exterior read in terms of alignment and proportion. Unless your plan is intended for a very warm climate, try to locate most of the windows on the south side and few, if any, on the north. South-facing windows allow for solar gain. North-facing windows allow for winter heat loss.

Along these same lines, be sure to provide seasonal shade for south-facing and west-facing windows. Deciduous trees work to this end, as their leaves provide summer shade and drop to reveal the winter sun. Awnings and porch roofs achieve the same effect by protecting windows from the relatively vertical rays of the summer sun while allowing the more horizontal rays inside.

Sliding doors, curtains and pocket doors can often save space as, they do not require an area in which to swing.

**Minimize throughways.** Hallways and oversized stairwells unnecessarily consume valuable space. If a stairway is required, consider making it a ladder. Paddle steps can also save space.

**Make use of  vertical space.** Shelves can usually go all the way to the ceiling; drawers can be put beneath the bed, cabinets can often be positioned over the table, and a sleeping loft may fit below a high ceiling.

**Consider using built-in furniture and storage in your design.** Freestanding furniture tends to leave awkward and unusable margins on both sides of where it is positioned. Built-ins generally stretch from wall-to-wall, and often floor-to-ceiling, to make use of every inch.

Built-ins are not only integral to a house in terms of function and structure, but in visual terms as well. Freestanding armoires, chests, and bookcases will fill up a small room quickly and tend to make any space feel more crowded. A wall of built-in cabinets can contain more possessions than all of these combined and comes off as far less visually intrusive. Built-in seating, cabinets, bookcases, work surfaces, and dining nooks can all be used to save and order space in this way.

Consider including some shallow shelves. Putting all of your glasses, vitamins and herbs on one deep shelf is going to demand that you dig for stuff that sits at the back. Less depth will put everything where you can get to it.

Carve out places near the door for the things that enter and leave your home: coat hooks, shoe cubbies, recycling bins, and the like.

**Keep it simple.** It is particularly important that a place for one be kept simple. For a single resident, all of the little extras can quickly add up to one big headache. The housing market currently offers very few properties designed specifically for one person. More often than not, those of us who choose to live alone end up saddled with the responsibilities of a house or apartment that was built for two or more residents.

Tumbleweed Tiny House Company's XS-House

The design of a single-occupancy dwelling is unique in that it requires relatively few, if any, interior walls. One room is often enough to contain everything that is necessary. Sometimes a separate little bathroom, kitchen, sleeping loft and/or closet can be useful, but the principal aim should be to keep things open. That said, it should be remembered that arbitrarily eliminating as many interior walls as possible will not necessarily result in a better space. While floor area and elbow room are inevitably gained, wall space is lost. This may affect the possibilities for furniture placement and storage options. Open-concept layouts are great so long as they truly correspond with the necessities at hand.

***Provide privacy and community.*** Designing a house for two or more people entails largely the same process, but the big room has to accommodate enough open space for all of the home's occupants to feel comfortable, and a small private area should be provided for every member of the household. Our need for a balance of both privacy and community is inherent, and if it is ignored in the design of a dwelling, strife will inevitably result. The private areas can be rooms, entire apartments within the structure, or even physically separate cottages. To increase the effectiveness of the private rooms within a house, closets should be located between them as sound buffers whenever it is possible.

These little private realms should be arranged around a shared larger area. One form that has been proven to work quite well as a shared space is the farmhouse kitchen mentioned earlier. In this case, the kitchen is also the dining room and the family/living room. It is designed to contain the dining table and cooking facilities, and enough space to serve a variety of functions.

In the common area of a shared household (be it inside or out), traffic zones and activity zones need to be kept apart. Unlike the space in a one-person residence or a private room, people will be passing through the common area regularly, so projects need to be kept out of traffic's way. Provide activity nodes at the area's periphery to keep the center wide open.

**Keep it light.** Light colors tend to make a space feel more open, while dark ones will make the same space feel crowded.

**Make it flexible.** If your desk can double as a dining table, so much the better. Mobile bookcases and cabinets can be used as room dividers, then moved out of the way for activities that require more space. A Murphy bed can transform an office into a guest room in seconds. Folding tables and chairs allow for further flexibility.

**Extend sight lines to make small rooms feel more generous.** Views from one part of the house into another or to the outdoors will make that part feel more expansive.

**Keep clutter out of sight and, thus, out of mind.** This goes a long way to improve how we experience a space. Be sure to include areas where clutter, or even everyday items, can be stored away and hidden from view. An uncluttered house will result in an uncluttered mind and unfettered creativity.

**Take advantage of the outdoors whenever possible.** Outdoor rooms add functional space without the added cost of water-tight, insulated construction.

***If necessary, sacrifice space for the illusion of space.*** Our perceptions of spaciousness often have more to do with perception itself than actual volume. Occasionally, it will become necessary to sacrifice actual space to achieve a design that feels more open. By lowering the ceiling in one area, for example, the volume in a neighboring area will generally appear to increase.

***Remember the invisible parts.*** With the basic shapes and sizes more or less established and in place, more attention can now be paid to arranging any furnishings or integral elements. Do not forget to include room for pipes and heating ducts if any are needed. Keep the plumbing as localized as possible. If the water heater is at one end of the house and the shower is at the other, you will have to wait a long while for hot water when you go to bathe.

***Keep refining.*** As the floor plan becomes clearer, feel free to add some details and to eliminate any unused or unusable parts. To read as a strong composition, every square inch of your house should be contributing to the whole structure and its function. Feet, inches and quarter-inches can be shaved off as the design begins to reveal its own needs. Before things get too finite on the inside, make scale drawings of the front, back and sides of the structure to determine what changes may need to be made there.

***Align everything that can be aligned.*** Consider the hierarchy of the place. Lower ceilings and enlarge some doorways, if necessary. So long as necessity is allowed to make the decisions, all of this should come pretty naturally. Remove yourself from the process and let nature take over. The resulting home will be beautifully simple.

# Basic Dimensions and Potential Restrictions

Every inch counts in a small house, so knowing exactly how many inches are required for each element is important. Dimensions for the integral parts of a house are listed here. The wall, floor and roof thicknesses listed are for the most standard type of construction—that which uses 2x lumber and half-inch plywood as the primary building materials. The greater the distance a rafter or joist needs to span, the thicker it and the roof or floor it comprises will need to be. A list of the most standard sizes for appliances and some considerably smaller options is also provided.

A house in Mendocino, CA

# Span Chart

RAFTER SPAN RATINGS (for roofs with a pitch over 3 in 12):

| SPECIES | 2 x 6 (16" o.c. / 24" o.c.) | 2 x 8 (16" o.c . / 24" o.c.) | 2 x 10 (16" o.c. / 24" o.c.) |
|---|---|---|---|
| Spruce/Pine/Fir No. 2 | 8'3" / 6'9" | 10'11" / 8'11" | 13'11" / 11'5" |
| Southern Pine No. 2 | 9'10" / 8'0" | 12'11" / 10'7" | 16'6" / 13'6" |
| Ponderosa Pine Sugar Pine | 8'1" / 6'8" | 10'9" / 8'9" | 13'9" / 11'3" |

FLOOR JOIST SPAN RATINGS:

| SPECIES | 2 x 8 (16" o.c. / 24" o.c.) | 2 x 10 (16" o.c. / 24" o.c.) | 2 x 12 (16" o.c. / 24" o.c.) |
|---|---|---|---|
| Dglas. Fir - Larch No. 2 | 13'1" / 11'3" | 16'9" / 14'5" | 20'4" / 17'6" |
| Dglas. Fir - South No. 2 | 12'0" / 10'6" | 15'3" / 13'4" | 18'7" / 16'3" |
| Ponderosa Pine/ Sugar Pine No. 2 | 11'4" / 9'3" | 14'5" / 11'9" | 17'7" / 14'4" |

Design Criteria: Strength—10-psf dead load plus 40-psf live load
Deflection—Limited to span in inches divided by 180
Source: National Lumber Manufacturers Association.

## Appliance Sizes

Refrigerator Dimensions:
    Avg. - 68 1/4" H x 29 3/4" W x 31 3/4" D
    Small – 34" H x 19" W x 20 1/2" D
    X-Small – 17" H x 19" W x 20 1/2" D
Range Dimensions:
    Avg. – 29 3/4" W x 46 1/2" H x 24"
    Small – 21 3/8" W x 16 11/16" H x 20" D (R.V. Style)
Washer:
    23 3/8" W x 33 1/4" H x 22 1/8" D
Dryer:
    23 3/8" W x 33 1/4" H x 22 1/8" D
Water Heater:
    6-Gallon – 17 3/4" H x 16" Diameter
    Tankless – 29 3/4" H x 18 1/4" W x 9" D
    12-Gallon – 22 3/4" H x 16" Diameter
Shower:
    Avg. – 30" W x 80" H x 30" D
    Small – 24" W x 72" H x 24" D
Tub:
    Avg. – 60" W x 18" H x 30" D
    Small – 48" W x 24" H x 30" D
Toilet:
    Avg. – 20" W x 29" H x 30" D
    Small – 18" W x 29" H x 24" D

## Anthropometric Data

More than 95% of U.S. adults are between 4'11" and 6'2" tall, with their shoes off. The average measures in at 5'7" (Architectural Graphic Standards). The remaining 5% have been excluded from the following data to keep it simple. If you or frequent visitors to your home are particularly tall or short, you may want to adjust accordingly. Ceiling heights and door widths have been calculated to fit a 6'2" person comfortably. Reach areas have been calculated for an unaided, 4'11" tall person. Work surface heights have been determined by what will most comfortably fit someone at the 5'7" median.

| | | |
|---|---|---|
| Ceiling Height: | 6'3" minimum | |
| Door Height: | 6'2" minimum | |
| Door Width: | 1'5" minimum | |
| Bed Width: | 2'8" minimum | |
| Bed Length: | 6'3" minimum | |
| Counter Height: | 2'8" minimum/ | 3'2" maximum |
| Counter Depth: | 1'4" minimum/ | 2'6" maximum |
| Door Knob Height: | 2'9" minimum/ | 3'4" maximum |
| Lavatory Height: | 2'6" minimum/ | 3'3" maximum |
| Control Knob Height: | 2'6" minimum/ | 6'0" maximum |
| High Shelf: | 6'2" maximum/ | |
| Desk/Table Height: | 1'0" minimum/ | 2'7" maximum |
| Desk/Table Depth: | 1'0" minimum/ | 2'8" maximum |
| Booth Width: | 5'0" minimum/ | 6'6" maximum |
| Sleeping Loft Height: | 2'10" minimum | |
| Leg Room Under Table: | 1'4" minimum | |
| Room or Hallway Width: | 1'8" minimum | |

## Codes and Regulations

Until building codes catch up with the environmental and social realities at hand, the question of how to meet or beat minimum-size standards remains. If guerilla housing, variances, or pushing to have your local codes changed hold no attraction, going with the flow may be your best bet. Most of the U.S. and Canada employ what is called the International Building Code. In spite of its name, the IBC is only really used in the U.S. and Canada. While the code is often tailored at the local level, it usually reads pretty much as listed here.

All houses shall have:
- At least one room of no less than 120 sq. ft.
- Ceilings of no less than 7 ft. (except 6'-8" in unfinished basements)
- No habitable room of less than 70 sq. ft. with no dimension smaller than 7' (except kitchens)
- A window (or second door) in every bedroom of no less than 5.7 sq. ft. total. Each must be at least 24" H x 20" W and no more than 44" above the floor
- A landing or floor on each side of all exterior doors that is no less than 36" deep x the width of the door
- Hallways of no less than 36" wide
- A door to the exterior that is no less than 36" W x 6'-8" H
- Egress for habitable basements (window wells of 9 sq. ft. or greater and 36" minimum any horizontal dimention
- Stairs of no less than 36" wide with 6'-8" headroom (except spiral stair-ways = 26" W x 78" H)
- Stairs with risers of no more than 7 3/4" and treads of no less than 10".

## Trailer Design Considerations (May vary by state)

- All trailers must have fenders or splashguards.
- When it is dark, all trailers must have stop lamps, a license plate light, and turn signals.
- Every trailer over 1500 pounds needs to be equipped with brakes.
- Trailers with brakes require an emergency brake system designed to activate in the event that the hitch fails.
- Tail lights are required (magnetic lights are okay).
- Trailers over 80" wide must have amber reflectors on each side and the front. Red reflectors are required in the rear.
- No vehicles in combination shall measure more than 65' in length.
- No vehicle may be wider than 102" without a special permit.
- Mirrors, lights, etc., may extend beyond 102", but not in excess of 10" on each side.
- No vehicle or load may exceed 13'-6" from pavement to top (14', some areas).

If you are making a corridor that is 20' wide, you can make it out out of concrete; if it is 10' wide, you should use stone; if it is 6' wide, use fine wood; but if it is is 2' wide, you should make it out of solid gold.
— *Carlo Scarpa*

# PART FOUR:
# PORTFOLIO OF HOUSES

Square feet: 172
House width: 8'-6"
House length: 20'
Road Height: 12'-3"
Dry Weight: 7000 lbs
Great Room: 9¼' x 5¼'
Kitchen: 5¼' x 4¾'
Bedroom: 7½' x 4¾'
Bathroom: 2' x 7¾'
Ceiling height: 7' 6"
-sizes are approximate

# POPOMO

The Popomo is different than my other portable homes in that it does not have a pronounced gabled roof or a loft. It does have a stainless steel boat fireplace, sink and stovetop, a refrigerator, wet bath, a full-sized bed, and a closet. The large glass wall is intended to face south during winter for excellent solar gain. The house is shown at right with hot rolled corrosion resistant steel siding and at left with the same siding and the wheels removed.

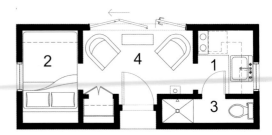

1. Kitchen    2.Bedroom    3.Bath
4.Great Room

Square feet: 65
House width: 7
House length: 11
Road Height: 12'-9"
Dry Weight: 3000 lbs
Porch: 2'x 1½'
Great Room: 4½' x 5½'
Kitchen: 4' x 4'
Bathroom: 3½' x 2'
Ceiling height: 6' 2"
Loft height: 3' 2"
-sizes are approximate

# XS-HOUSE

With a couch, a stainless steel desk, sink and fireplace, a wet bath, two closets and lots of shelving, plus a sleeping loft above, this portable structure was designed to house one full-time resident comfortably. A small refrigerator below the counter and a hot-plate are also included. If you were to count the loft, this house would actually be about 130 square feet.

1. Great Room  2. Kitchen  3. Wet Bath  4. Loft.

Square feet:     89
House width:     8'
House length:   15'
Road Height:    13'-5"
Dry Weight:     4700 lbs
Porch:          3' x 7½'
Great Room:     6' x 6½'
Kitchen:        4' x 4½'
Bathroom:       4' x 2'
Ceiling height: 6' 6"
Loft height:    3' 8"
-sizes are approximate

# EPU

Epu is the design I came up with for my house. It features a stainless steel desk, a tiny fireplace, a refrigerator, sink, stovetop, wet bath, a full-sized bed, plenty of storage and integral wheels. The 89 square feet listed do not include the porch or sleeping loft. It is shown here with an optional Gothic window.

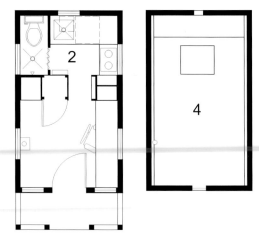

1. Great Room  2. Kitchen  3. Wet Bath  4. Loft.

Square feet:      102
House width:      8'
House length:    15'
Road Height:     13'-5"
Dry Weight:       4900 lbs
Porch:             2½'x 2½'
Great Room:      6' x 6½'
Kitchen:           4' x 4½'
Bathroom:         4' x 2'
Ceiling height:    6' 6"
Loft height:       3' 8"
-sizes are approximate

# WEEBEE

The Weebee is much like the Epu design with the addition of a Dutch hip roof and a bump-out downstairs. The 102 square feet listed only refer to the downstairs and not the porch or loft. This tiny abode comes on integral wheels. The bump-out fits a table or a couch that folds out into a bed.

1. Great Room  2. Kitchen  3. Wet Bath  4. Loft.

141

Square feet:      89
House width:      12'
House length:     9'
Dry Weight:       4700 lbs
Porch:            3' x 1½'
Great Room:       6' x 6½'
Kitchen:          4' x 4½'
Bathroom:         4' x 2'
Ceiling height: 6' 6"
Loft height:      3' 8"

sizes are approximate

# BURNHARDT

The Burnhardt is essentialy the Epu turned sideways. It includes all of the same amenities but no wheels.

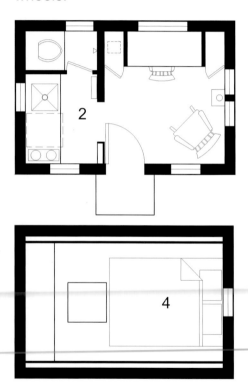

1. Great Room  2. Kitchen  3. Wet Bath  4. Loft.

Square feet: 117
House width: 8'
House length: 19'
Road Height: 13'-5"
Dry Weight: 5400 lbs
Porch: 3'x 7½'
Great Room: 6' x 6½'
Kitchen: 6' x 6½'
Bathroom: 3' x 6'
Ceiling height: 0' 0"/10' 6"
Loft height: 3' 8"
-sizes are approximate

# LUSBY

The Lusby has a full bathroom, a kichen (sink, stovetop, refrig-erator), a fireplace, two closets, ample shelving, a downstairs bed-room and two lofts for additional sleeping and/or storage. The great room has a high, cathedral ceiling. In addition to the 117 square feet listed, this house contains more than 60 square feet in the lofts.

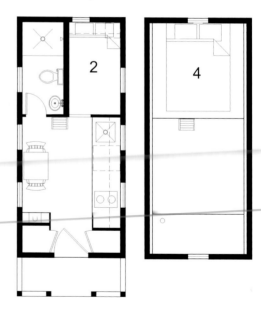

1. Kitchen/Living  2. Bedroom  3. Bath  4. Loft  5. Storage.

Square feet: 117
House width: 8'
House length: 19'
Road Height: 13'-5"
Dry Weight: 5400 lbs
Porch: 3'x 7½'
Great Room: 6' x 6½'
Kitchen: 3½' x 6½'
Bathroom: 3' x 6'
Ceiling height: 6' 6"/10' 6"
Loft height: 3' 8"
-sizes are approximate

## TARLETON

The Tarleton has the same over-all footprint and exterior appearance as the Lusby. The primary differences inside are that the Tarleton's kitchen is a bit bigger and that there is no bedroom downstairs. The loft space is the same.

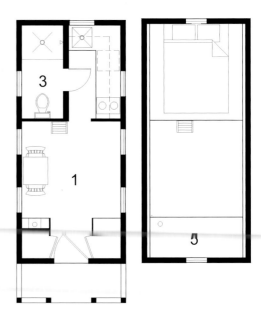

1. Great Room  2. Kitchen  3. Bath
4. Loft  5. Storage.

159

Square feet:      130
House width:      8'
House length:    19'
Road Height:     13'-5"
Dry Weight:       5400 lbs
Porch:               3'x 7½'
Great Room:      6' x 6½'
Kitchen:            3½' x 6½'
Bathroom:          3' x 0'
Ceiling height:  6' 6"/10' 6"
Loft height:       3' 8"
-sizes are approximate

# FENCL

The Fencl (pronounced fen-sel) is a combination of the Tarleton and the Weebee. There is a tall cathedral ceiling over the great room and lofts over the bathroom, kitchen and doorway. Like the Weebee, this house has a bump-out to accommodate a fold-out bed or a table.

1. Great Room  2. Kitchen  3. Bath
4. Loft  5. Storage.

Square feet:      261
With add-on:     356
House width:     14'
House length:    24'
Porch:           6' x 13¼'
Great Room:      9' x 13¼'
Kitchen:         7¾' x 8'
Bathroom:        7¾' x 5'
Addition:        7' x 9¾'
Ceiling height: 7' 6"
Loft height:     7' 6"
-sizes are approximate

# BODEGA

The Bodega has a fireplace, a full bath and kitchen and a washer/dryer beneath the counter. I don't count the loft as square footage in this house because, with so much sloped ceiling, it doesn't officially qualify as a habitable room. That said, with seven feet of ceiling height over more than 70 square feet, this heated loft provides a lot of usable space.

1. Great Room  2. Kitchen  3. Bath
4. Loft.

Square feet:        297
With add-on:        391
House width:        14'
House length:       24'
Porch:              6' x 6'
Great Room:         9' x 13 ¼'
Kitchen:            7¾' x 8'
Bathroom:           7¾' x 5'
Addition:           7' x 9¾'
Ceiling height:     7' 6"
Loft height:        7'
-sizes are approximate

# HARBINGER

The Harbinger is the Dutch hip version of the Bodega described on page 168. In this case, a bump-out provides enough space for an additional bedroom or sitting room downstairs. If one were to count the loft, this house would actually measure almost 600 square feet, or 700, with the add-on.

1. Great Room  2. Sitting Room  3. Kitchen  4. Bath  5. Loft.

Square feet: 278
With add-on: 372
House width: 20'
House length: 20'
Porch: 6' x 13½'
Great Room: 9' x 13'
Kitchen: 7½' x 7½'
Bathroom: 5½' x 5½'
Addition: 9¾' x 7'
Ceiling height: 7' 6"
Loft height: 7'
sizes are approximate

# NEW VESICA

The New Vesica is essentially the Bodega turned sideways. The New Vesica is officially 278 square feet, but, if the loft were included, it would measure in at just over 450 square feet.

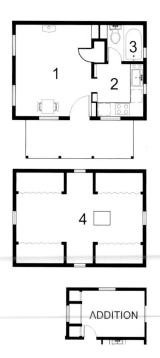

1. Great Room  2. Kitchen  3. Bath  4. Loft.

Square feet:     261
With add-on:     356
House width:     14'
House length:    24'
Porch:           6' x 13¼'
Great Room:      9' x 13¼'
Kitchen:         7¾' x 8'
Bathroom:        7¾' x 5'
Addition:        7' x 9¾'
Ceiling height:  7' 6"
Loft height:     7'
-sizes are approximate

# Loring

The Loring is the same as the Bodega except that, in this case, I have added a small bump-out in the loft. Once again, the loft is not counted in the square footage listed but contains ample space. A downstairs bedroom is also avalable.

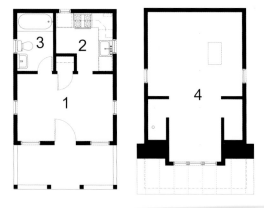

ADDITION

1. Great Room  2. Kitchen  3. Bath  4. Loft.

Square feet: 681
With add-on: 774
House width: 16'
House length: 30'
Porch: 6' x 15½'
Great Room: 9½' x 15'
Kitchen: 7½' x 9½'
Bathroom: 5½' x 6'
Half Bath: 4½' x 5'
Addition: 7' x 12'
Ceiling height: 7' 6"
-sizes are approximate

# Enesti

The Enesti, or NST (not so tiny), contains two bedrooms, one-and a-half baths, a fireplace, a dining nook, ample storage and a full kitchen that includes a washer/ dryer beneath the counter. A third bedroom is also available.

1. Great Room  2. Kitchen  3. Half Bath  4. Full Bath  5. BR-1  6. BR-2

Square feet: 681
With add-on: 774
House width: 24'
House length: 22'
Porch: 6' x 18'
Great Room: 9½' x 15½'
Kitchen: 7½' x 9½'
Bathroom: 5½' x 6'
Half Bath: 4½' x 5'
Addition: 7' x 12'
Ceiling height: 7' 6"
-sizes are approximate

# Sebastorosa

The layout of the Sebastorosa is basically the same as the Enesti tuned sideways.

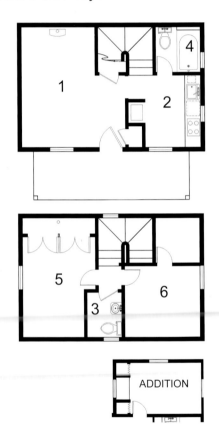

1. Great Room  2. Kitchen  3. Half Bath  4. Full Bath 5. BR-1, 6. BR-2

Square feet:      743
With add-on:      837
House width:      16'
House length:     30'
Porch:            6' x 15½'
Great Room:       9½' x 15'
Kitchen:          7½' x 9½'
Bathroom:         5½' x 6'
Half Bath:        4½' x 5'
Addition:         7' x 12'
Ceiling height: 7' 6"
-sizes are approximate

# B-53

The B-53 is the biggest design I offer. It is essentially the Enesti with a bungalow exterior and a bump-out over the porch.

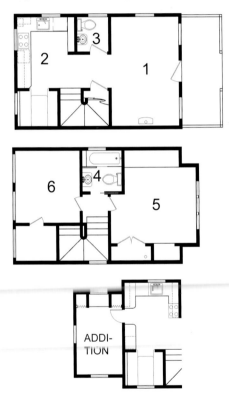

1. Great Room  2. Kitchen  3. Half Bath  4. Full Bath 5. BR-1  6. BR-2

Square feet: 390
House width: 28'
House length: 14'
Great Room: 10' x 12'
Kitchen: 7' x 8'
Bathroom: 5' x 5'
Ceiling height: 8'
-sizes are approximate

## Z-Glass House

This contemporary design does not have a pronounced gabled roof or loft. It looks a lot like the New Popomo, but is about three times bigger. Like its smaller cousin, the Z-Glass House has a glass wall that is intended to face south during the winter for solar gain. This design includes a stainless steel counter, sink, range and refrigerator, a full bath and a fireplace. While it is not built on integral wheels, it is small enough to be moved on a trailer. It is shown at right with hot rolled steel siding.

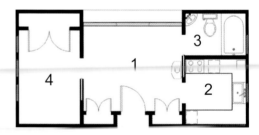

1. Great Room  2. Kitchen  3. Bath
4. Bedroom.

Square feet:        461
With add-on:        557
House width:        16'
House length:       30'
Porch:              6' x 6'
Great Room:         10' x 15¼'
Kitchen:            7¼' x 7'
Bathroom:           7¼' x 4½'
Addition:           7' x 10'
Ceiling height:     7' 0"
-sizes are approximate

# Whidbey

The Whidbey's main floor is similar to that of the B-53 and Enesti, except that it uses a bump-out to house a downstairs bedroom, and it has a full main floor bathroom, including a sink over the toilet. Pictured below is the add-on version with 2 bedrooms. I do not count the upstairs 400+ square feet because, with so much sloped ceiling, it does not officially qualify as a habitable room.

1. Great Room, 2. Kitchen, 3. Full Bath 4. ,Bedroom 5. Loft.

Square feet:    63
House width:    7'
House length:   10'
Ceiling height:  9' 6"
-sizes are approximate

## Biensi

This tiny structure, and those following it, are different than the ones on the preceeding pages. Inside you will find a single open room.  Just add closet(s), a loft, utilities and furniture as needed. The pictures on the following pages show how my friend Greg managed to fit everything he needs to live full-time in his Biensi.  Visit www.resourcesforlife and click on "mobile hermiage" for more about Greg and his house.

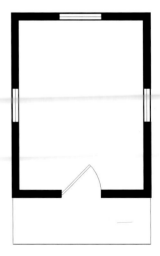

Square feet:   89
House width:   8'
House length: 15'
Road Height:  13'-5"
Dry Weight:   4400 lbs
Porch:        3'x 7½'
Ceiling height: 6'-3"
-sizes are approximate

## Wildflower

The Wildflower is like my house on the outside with a single, open room inside. Add closet(s), a loft, utilities, furniture and entire rooms as you see fit.

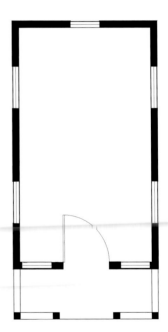

Square feet:    117
House width:    8'
House length:   19'
Road Height:    13'-5"
Dry Weight:     5100 lbs
Porch:          3' x 7½'
Ceiling height: 6'-3"
-sizes are approximate

# Ofnoco

The exterior of the Ofnoco resembles the Tarleton and the Lusby. The inside is a blank slate with space to create a tiny home of your own.

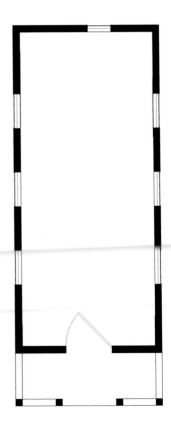

## Vardo

The Vardo is not much more than a full-sized bed flanked by a couple of work surfaces over 35 cubic feet of storage space. It can be pulled behind virtually any car or removed from its trailer to rest in most any truck bed. It is pictured on these pages with an optional fireplace.

Square feet:     36
House width:    6'
House length:  6½'
Road Height:   6'-5"
Dry Weight:    950 lbs
Ceiling height: 4'-3"
-sizes are approximate

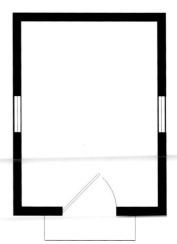

# Plans

The plans pictured here are for the Lusby. Those for the rolling houses include instructions for attaching the house to the trailer. Please visit tumbleweedhouses.com for more information.

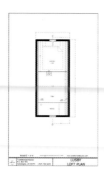

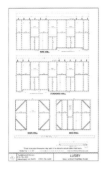

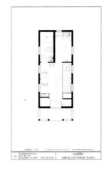
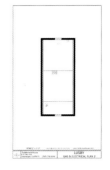

# Endnotes

1. *Worldwatch Paper 124*, by D. M. Roodman and N. Lenssen, Worldwatch Institute, Washington, D.C., 1996.
2. NPR's *cartalk.com* interview with Adam Stein and Tom Boucher.
3. U.S. Bureau of the Census.
4. National Association of Home Builders. $244,000 is the average price of all houses sold in August, 2008.
5. *How Buildings Learn*, by Stewart Brand, Viking Press, 1994.
6. Iowa City Building Codes.
7. *Residential Street Typology and Injury Accident Frequency,* by Peter Swift Associates, 1997.

# About the Author

Jay Shafer is leading a movement that is changing the way America views housing. His revolutionary approach to house design has stirred international dialogue. In his, *The Small House Book* (self-published, 2000), Shafer explains why smaller dwellings make good sense and how superior design can be achieved with less space. He has continued to share his philosophy by creating Tumbleweed Tiny House Company through such venues as *Fine Homebuilding, The Wall Street Journal, The Oprah Winfrey Show,* and at the University of Iowa's School

of Art, where he served as Adjunct Assistant Professor of Drawing for more than a decade. Professor Shafer currently lives in a 89 square foot home of his own creation.

Visit www.tumbleweedhouses.com for more about Jay and Tumbleweed Tiny House Company.

# Endorsements

*"A visionary designer…"* – Catherine Halley, <u>Domino Magazine</u>

*"…guru of the small house movement."* – John Blackstone, <u>CBS Sunday</u>

*"…part of a new generation of cutting-edge designers."* – Aric Chen, <u>Paper</u>

*"…instant curb appeal."* – Bethany Little, <u>New York Times</u>

*"…one hundred square feet of bliss."* – Thelma Gutierrez, <u>CNN</u>

*"…a monument to life pared to its essence."* – Dan Weeks, <u>Living Room</u>

*"…built to last."* – Craig LaMoult, <u>Chicago Tribune</u>

*"…an efficient use of every inch of space."* – Cheryl Corley, <u>NPR</u>

*"…astounding…"* – Oprah Whinfrey, <u>The Oprah Winfrey Show</u>

*"…extraordinary attention to detail."* – Hannah Bloch, <u>New York Times</u>

*"…an inspiration…"* – Christopher Solomon, <u>MSN Real Estate</u>

*"…designed to last a lifetime."* – Julie Martin, <u>BBC News</u>

*"Move-in-ready gems…"* –Denise Gee, <u>Better Homes & Gardens</u>

*"…a testament to discriminating taste".* – Carol Loyd, <u>San Francisco Gate</u>